KU-168-034

Jill Lepore is the David Woods Kemper '41 Professor of American History at Harvard University and a staff writer at The New Yorker. Her many books include *The Secret History of Wonder Woman*, a national bestseller, *Book of Ages*, a finalist for the National Book Award and *These Truths: A History of the United States*. She lives in Cambridge, Massachusetts.

THIS
AMERICA

The Case for the Nation

JILL LEPORE

JOHN MURRAY

First published in the United States in 2019 by Liveright
Publishing Corporation, a division of W. W. Norton & Company, Inc.
First published in Great Britain in 2019 by John Murray (Publishers)
An Hachette UK company

This paperback edition published in 2020

1

A CIP catalogue record for this title is available from the British Library

This book began with an essay published in *Foreign Affairs*
(March/April 2019) as "A New Americanism." It also borrows—
and takes its title—from a short essay, "This America," that
appeared in *The New Yorker* (12 November 2018).

Paperback ISBN 9781529386110
eBook ISBN 9781529386127

Typeset in Fairfield LT Std

Printed and bound in Great Britain by Clays Ltd, Elcograf S.p.A.

John Murray policy is to use papers that are natural, renewable and
recyclable products and made from wood grown in sustainable forests.
The logging and manufacturing processes are expected to conform to the
environmental regulations of the country of origin.

John Murray (Publishers)
Carmelite House
50 Victoria Embankment
London EC4Y 0DZ

www.johnmurraypress.co.uk

In memory of my father,
whose immigrant parents
named him Amerigo in 1924,
the year Congress passed a law
banning immigrants like them

Nations reel and stagger on their way; they make hideous mistakes; they commit frightful wrongs; they do great and beautiful things. And shall we not best guide humanity by telling the truth about all this, so far as the truth is ascertainable?

—W. E. B. DuBois,
"The Propaganda of History," 1935

THIS LITTLE BOOK undertakes three outsized tasks, things that haven't been done much lately, things that seemed to me in need of doing. It explains the origins of nations. It offers a brief history of American nationalism. And it makes the case for the nation, and for the enduring importance of the United States and of American civic ideals, by arguing against nationalism, and for liberalism.

A long essay, really, this book is at once an argument and a plea, a reckoning with American history, the nation at its worst, and a call for a new Americanism, as tough- minded and openhearted as the nation at its best.

THIS AMERICA

HISTORY
AND NATIONS

———————

Nations are made up of people but held together by history, like wattle and daub or lath and plaster or bricks and mortar. For a generation, American history has been coming undone and the nation has been coming apart, the daub cracking, the plaster buckling, the mortar crumbling. This tragedy was foreseen.

In 1986, the Pulitzer Prize–winning, bow-tie-wearing Stanford historian Carl N. Degler delivered something other than the usual pipe-smoking, Scotch-on-the-rocks after-dinner disquisition that had plagued the evening program of the annual meeting of the American Historical Association for nearly all of its century-long history. Instead, Degler, a gentle and quietly heroic man, accused his colleagues of nothing short of dereliction of duty: appalled by nationalism, they had abandoned the study of the nation.

"We can write history that implicitly denies or

ignores the nation-state, but it would be a history that flew in the face of what people who live in a nation-state require and demand," Degler said that night, in Chicago, in a speech titled "In Pursuit of an American History." He issued a warning: "If we historians fail to provide a nationally defined history, others less critical and less informed will take over the job for us."

Degler was worried about his contemporaries, intellectuals who had stopped studying the nation, believing that the nation-state was on the decline. The world had grown global, tied together by intricate webs of trade and accelerating forms of transportation and communication. The future was cosmopolitan, they insisted, not provincial. Why bother to study the nation?

Many of Degler's contemporaries also believed that studying the nation would prop up nationalism, which ought, instead, be left to die. By the last quarter of the twentieth century nationalism was, outside of postcolonial states, nearly dead, a stumbling, ghastly wraith. And many intellectuals believed that if they stopped writing national history, nationalism would die sooner, starved, neglected, deserted, a fitting death for a war criminal, destroyer of worlds.

Francis Fukuyama's much-read 1989 essay "The

End of History?" appeared three years after Degler delivered his speech, but it remains the best-known illustration of the wisdom of Degler's warning. At the end of the Cold War, Fukuyama announced that fascism and communism were dead and that nationalism, seemingly all but the last threat to liberalism left standing, was utterly decrepit in Europe ("European nationalism has been defanged") and that, where it was still kicking in other parts of the world, well, that wasn't quite nationalism: it was a halting striving for democracy.

But nationalism did not die. It ravaged Bosnia and Rwanda. It carried to positions of influence and power, even murderous power, nationalists including Vladimir Putin in Russia, Recep Tayyip Erdoğan in Turkey, Viktor Orbán in Hungary, Marine Le Pen in France, Jaroslaw Kaczynski in Poland, and Rodrigo Duterte in the Philippines. Three decades after Degler issued his warning, Britain voted to leave the European Union and the United States elected Donald Trump, who went on to declare, "I'm a nationalist, okay?" In a new book, Fukuyama retreated from many of his earlier claims, insisting that in 1989 he had never exactly said that nationalism was "about to disappear." But Fukuyama had been hardly alone in pronouncing nationalism all but dead in the 1980s. A lot of other people had, too. That's what troubled Carl Degler. Degler didn't think nationalism was about to go away, and he was worried that if intellectuals kept thinking it would, they'd keep ignoring it, and they'd not only fail to fight it, they'd lose the ability to fight it, like a boxer out of training, flabby, slow-footed, and fainthearted.

Nation-states, when they form, imagine a past. Modern historical writing arose with the nation-state. So did modern liberalism. From the founding of the United States until the 1960s, the subject of American history was the study of the American nation. Over that same stretch of time, the United States waged wars of conquest across the continent, fell into a civil war, fought two world wars, and entered a cold war, while a people held in bondage fought for their emancipation only to face a legal regime of segregation and a vigilante campaign of terrorism, leading to a decades-long struggle for civil rights, even as the United States became the leader of a liberal world order. If American historians didn't always succeed in affirming a common history during these tumultuous years—and they didn't—they nevertheless engaged in the struggle, offering appraisals and critiques of national aims and ends, advancing arguments, fostering debate, defending democracy, and celebrating, often lyrically, the beauty of the land, the inventiveness of the people, and the vitality of American ideals. And so, each in a different way, did the people left out of those national histories, women and people of color who fought for freedom and sovereignty and citizenship and equality and justice, and who also fought their way into the academy.

In the 1970s, the historical profession broadened; so did American history. Studying the nation fell out of favor. Instead, most academic historians looked at either smaller or bigger things, investigating groups—divided by race, sex, or class—or taking the vantage promised by global history. They produced excellent scholarship, meticulously researched and brilliantly argued accounts of the lives and struggles and triumphs of Americans that earlier generations of historians had ignored. They studied peoples within nations and ties across nations. And, appalled by nationalism, they disavowed national history, as nationalism's handmaiden. But when scholars stopped writing national history, other, less scrupulous people stepped in.

Nations, to make sense of themselves, need some

kind of agreed-upon past. They can get it from scholars or they can get it from demagogues, but get it they
will. The endurance of nationalism proves that there's
never any shortage of fiends and frauds willing to
prop up people's sense of themselves and their destiny with a tissue of myths and prophecies, prejudices
and hatreds, or to pour out the contents of old rub-
bish bags full of festering incitements, resentments,
and calls to violence. When serious historians aban-
don the study of the nation, when scholars stop trying
to write a common history for a people, nationalism
doesn't die. Instead, it eats liberalism.

Liberalism is still in there. The trick is getting it out.
There's only one way to do that. It requires grabbing
and holding onto a very good idea: that all people are
equal and endowed from birth with inalienable rights
and entitled to equal treatment, guaranteed by a nation
of laws. This requires making the case for the nation.

· II ·

NATIONS
AND NATIONALISM

The United States is different from other nations and its nationalism is different, too. Every nation is different from every other: nations define themselves by their differences, even when they have to invent them; that's part of what makes them nations. The world hasn't always been divided into nations and there's no reason to believe it always will be, not least because the most pressing problem confronting the world—climate change—is planetary. It's possible to imagine a world without nations. In the meantime, that world does not exist, and this world is a world of nations, which is why it's important to understand what nations are, and to imagine what they can be.

The idea of a nation is very old, an artifact of antiquity. "Nation" has the same Latin root as "nativity," meaning birth. A nation, historically, is a people who share a common descent. In Genesis, the families of the sons of Noah are "divided in their lands; every one after his tongue, after their families, in their nations."

Medieval European universities were divided into "nations" by language and origin. Seventeenth-century English colonists used the word "nation" to refer to people like the Haudenosaunee, a centuries-old confederation of Iroquois that the English called the Five Nations. Over the course of the eighteenth century, "nation" began to mean something tied more closely to sovereignty and power. "Our wise Forefathers established Union and Amity between the Five Nations," Canasatego, an Onondaga leader, told English colonists in 1744. "This has made us formidable."

Nationalism, though, is not a very old idea. It is an artifact of modernity. "Nationalism," the word, wasn't coined until the end of the eighteenth century, and the thing itself didn't really emerge until well into the nineteenth century, and then mainly in Europe. It meant both a conviction that the world is and ought to be divided into nations and a particular emotional attachment to your own.

Sometimes people confuse nationalism with patriotism. There's nothing wrong and all kinds of things right with loving the place where you live and the people you live with and wanting that place and those people to thrive, so it's easy to confuse nationalism and patriotism, especially because they once meant

more or less the same thing. But by the early decades
of the twentieth century, with the rise of fascism in
Europe, nationalism had come to mean something
different from patriotism, something fierce, something violent: less a love for your own country than
a hatred of other countries and their people and a
hatred of people within your own country who don't
belong to an ethnic, racial, or religious majority.
Immigration policy is a topic for political debate; reasonable people disagree. But hating immigrants, as
if they were lesser humans, is a form of nationalism
that has nothing to do with patriotism. Trade policy
is a topic for political debate; reasonable people disagree. But hating globalists, as if they were fiends,
is a form of nationalism that has nothing to do with
patriotism.

Confusing nationalism and patriotism is not always
innocent. Louis Snyder, a City College of New York
professor who witnessed the rise of Nazism in Germany in the 1920s, once explained why, in a book
called *The Meaning of Nationalism*. Nationalists,
he observed, "have a vested interest in maintaining
a vagueness of language as a cloak for their aims."
Because it's difficult to convince people to pursue a
course of aggression, violence, and domination, requir-

ing sacrifices made in the name of the nation, nationalists pretend their aims are instead protection and unity and that their motivation is patriotism. This is a lie. Patriotism is animated by love, nationalism by hatred. To confuse the one for the other is to pretend that hate is love and fear is courage.

Nationalism, an infant in the nineteenth century, became, in the first half of the twentieth, a monster—the rage behind der Führer and Il Duce, bigoted and brutal, violent and finally genocidal. In the middle decades of the twentieth century, nationalism swept many parts of Africa, Asia, and Latin America. But during those same decades, Europe reeled from the havoc wrought by nationalism, which is why Fukuyama was able to argue, in 1989, that nationalism in Europe had been "defanged," and that nationalism in other parts of the world was less an ideology than a means to achieving independence. Only at the very fringes did political figures in the West any longer call themselves "nationalists."

That changed early in the twenty-first century, when nationalists stopped mincing words. "We're putting America first and it hasn't happened in a lot of decades," Donald Trump said at a rally in Houston, Texas, in the fall of 2018, before a crowd sixteen thousand strong. "We're taking care of ourselves for a change, folks," he said, nodding his head. Supporters waved KEEP AMERICA GREAT signs and FINISH THE WALL placards. He warned of a conspiracy designed to "restore the rule of corrupt, power-hungry globalists." The crowd booed. "You know what a globalist is, right? A globalist is a person that wants the globe to do well, frankly, not caring about our country so much. And you know what? We can't have that. You know, they have a word, it sort of became old-fashioned—it's called a 'nationalist.' And I say, really, we're not supposed to use that word. You know what I am?" He poked his chest. "I'm a nationalist, okay?" The crowd roared. "I'm a nationalist!" His voice rose. "Use that word! *Use that word!*"

Merriam-Webster reported that between the day of Trump's Houston speech and the day after, online dictionary searches for the definition of the word "nationalism" rose by 8,000 percent, ranking the word among the top ten most looked-up of the year 2018. Talking with reporters at the White House the day after his Houston speech, Trump professed both ignorance of the history of nationalism and indifference. He said with a shrug, "I think it should be brought back." It should not.

· III ·

NATIONS
AND STATES

Nationalism is a by-product of the nation-state. A state is a political community, governed by laws; a nation-state is a political community, governed by laws, that, at least theoretically, unites a people who share common origins, as if they were a family. In practice, though, a nation-state does not ordinarily unite a people who share common descent by geography and birth; instead it gathers together all sorts of people, from many different places and lines of descent, speaking different languages, attached to different traditions, and belonging to different faiths. Sometimes, when this happens, a powerful majority purges its population of minorities, by massacre, imprisonment, persecution, or deportation. The Catholic monarchs of fifteenth-century and sixteenth-century Spain, for instance, slaughtered and banished Muslims and Jews. More often, as nation-states emerged out of city-states and kingdoms and empires, they instead incorporated all of the different people living in newly bounded territories, and the best way to do that was to invent a common history, telling tales about a shared past, tying together ribbons of facts and myths, as if everyone in the "English nation" had the same ancestors, when in truth they were everything from Celts to Saxons. Histories of nation-states are stories that hide the seams that stitch the nation to the state.

Nationalism, when it emerged, was a product of the Enlightenment, and a species of liberalism. To be a nationalist at the end of the eighteenth century meant to believe in a slew of revolutionary liberal ideas: that the peoples of the world are naturally divided into nations, that the most rational means of government is national self-rule, that nations are sovereign, and that nations guarantee the rights of citizens. Nationalism was first expressed not in the United States but in Europe and is usually dated not to the American Revolution but to the French one, and especially to France's 1789 Declaration of the Rights of Man and the Citizen: "The principle of any sovereignty resides essentially in the Nation; no body of men, no individual, can exercise authority that does not emanate expressly from it." Politics became the operation of a new force, not the divine right of kings but the will of the nation.

American nationalism is and always has been complicated, so complicated that it has been said that "nationalism is unknown" in the United States. This isn't true—in fact it's ludicrous—but American nationalism is distinctive, in part, because of the strange manner in which the nation was formed.

The United States began not as a nation but as a confederation of thirteen states and, before that, a collection of colonies. The land had for tens of thousands of years been inhabited by people originally from Asia. It had then been seized, conquered, and settled by people from Europe who brought with them people from Africa, held in bondage. The thirteen colonies they established had little in common, so little that in 1775 John Adams remarked that they differed almost "as much as several distinct Nations." The devising of an American "nation" out of that past is pushing a cart uphill.

In 1776, the world began all over again, as Thomas Paine put it: "A situation, similar to the present, hath not happened since the days of Noah until now. The birthday of a new world is at hand." The shackles of tyranny were cast off. A colonized people declared their independence. Subjects to a king became a free people. They declared themselves to be born equal, each endowed with rights that no one could take away. Time stopped, and began again.

"We hold these truths to be self-evident: that all men are created equal, that they are endowed by their creator with certain inalienable rights; that among these are life, liberty, and the pursuit of happiness." For all its soaring, hallowed prose, the Declaration of Independence never described the United States as a nation and it invoked not national but universal ideas.

The Articles of Confederation, a treaty drafted in 1777, tied together the thirteen former colonies, now states, in a "confederation and perpetual union," not unlike the Iroquois confederacy, and guaranteed their sovereignty under "a firm league of friendship"; there, too, the word "nation" did not appear, except in reference to possible attack by "some nation of Indians." The American Revolution was an extraordinary turning point in the history of the world, a new beginning. But it had little to do with the idea of an American nation.

Long after the Revolution, most Americans perceived of the United States not as a nation but, true to its name, as a confederation of states. This even manifested itself grammatically. For decades, the country's name was a plural noun. The United States *are*, not the United States *is*. What, then, made this bundle of states a nation? Not the Constitution, drafted in 1787, which was so fragile that it's aptly been called a "roof without walls." That roof without walls had a dungeon in its cellar. Its polity was unequal; for purposes of representation, it excluded "Indians not taxed" (that is, indigenous peoples living in their own nations) and counted enslaved people (people of African descent held as chattel) at three-fifths of the rate by which it counted an invented category of "white people."

Like the Declaration of Independence and the Articles of Confederation, the Constitution never called the United States a "nation." Its advocates, led by Alexander Hamilton, James Madison, and John Jay, called themselves Federalists, not national-ists, even though, in fact, they were nationalists, in the sense that they were proposing to replace a fed-eral government, under the Articles of Confederation, with a national government. Knowing only too well that many Americans, like Virginia's Patrick Henry, objected to a national government but favored a fed-eral one, the Federalists' decision to call themselves "Federalists" was an act of political genius, since it left their frustrated opponents, who were, in fact, federal-ists, to labor under the label "Anti-Federalists."

The Constitution asked the states to give up some of their authority to a new, national government. The citizens of the early United States were Virginians and Pennsylvanians and Marylanders and Georgians. Were they Americans? Not so much. Why would people attached to their states but not very attached to the nation agree to a national government? Federalists mainly concentrated their efforts on explaining the benefits of the Constitution, especially the political stability it promised to provide. That stability rested on a compromise that allowed not only for the continuation of slavery in the South, at a time when it was on the wane in the North, but also for the granting of disproportionate political power to slave states, in exchange for their willingness to stay in the Union. As for the problem of a lack of national attachment, Federalists mostly pretended that it wasn't actually a problem. New York's John Jay insisted, in Federalist No. 2, "that Providence has been pleased to give this one connected country to one united people—a people descended from the same ancestors, speaking the same language, professing the same religion, attached to the same principles of government, very similar in their manners and customs."

Ratification was a closely fought battle. After they

won it, Federalists undertook to promote the very sense
of national belonging that Jay had pretended already
existed. And so, in the spirit of unifying the country,
did their early opponents, the Anti-Federalists, now
more or less reconstituted as Jeffersonian Republicans. Americans began holding Fourth of July parades,
at once celebrating their independence and fostering
national attachment. In 1789, Jedidiah Morse published *American Geography, Or, a View of the Present Situation of the United States of America*, in order
to cultivate and nourish a national feeling. "Like the
Nation of which it treats," Morse explained, his book
was "but an infant, and, as such, solicits the fostering care of the country it describes." Noah Webster
attempted to manufacture a national character by urging Americans to adopt distinctive spelling. His first,
short dictionary appeared in 1806. "Language, as well
as government, should be national," Webster wrote.
"America should have her *own*, distinct from all the
world." That got the United States "favor" instead of
"favour." It did not, however, make the United States
a nation. "We are all Republicans, we are all Federalists," Jefferson proclaimed in his inaugural address
in 1801, urging a spirit of Americanism. Nothing so
stirred early feelings of American nationalism as much

as the War of 1812. And yet, in 1825, when Webster finished compiling his monumental two-volume *American Dictionary of the English Language*, he did not include the word "nationalism." But a year later, in 1826, when Americans celebrated the fiftieth anniversary of the Declaration of Independence, a sense of national attachment really had begun to develop, a half century late, walls under that roof.

The United States, in other words, was a state before it became a nation. This course of events is so unusual—a state forming before it becomes a nation, rather than a nation forming and then becoming a state—that it's useful to think of the United States not as a nation-state but instead as something stranger, a state-nation, a thing as rare as hens' teeth.

· IV ·

THE EMERGENCE OF NATIONALISM

The language of nationalism, when it surfaced in the United States in the 1830s, had less to do with feel-

ings of national belonging than with the ongoing dis-
pute between federal power and states' rights. To be a
nationalist meant to advocate for the power of the federal government. After the Federalist Party died, the
National Republican Party, founded in 1824, briefly
replaced it. Its members were known as the "Nation-
als," and what they advocated was nationalism. When
the National Party ticket did poorly in Massachusetts
in 1831, one newspaper joked that "we might infer
that 'nationalism' is in a bad way, even in Boston."

Against nationalists stood both sectionalists, who
opposed any call for an end to slavery as a violation of
states' rights, and native peoples, who refused to recognize the jurisdictional claims of the federal government. "This spirit of sectionalism must be supplanted
with that of nationalism," cried nationalists. Down
with nationalism, cried sectionalists. "Everything, Mr.
President, is running into nationality," Virginia senator John Tyler fumed on the floor of the Senate in
1833. "You cannot walk along the streets without see-
ing the word on every sign—national hotel, national
boot-black, national black-smith, national oyster-
house." All this was by way of introduction to Tyler's
argument, advocating states' rights: "The Government
was created by the States, is amenable by the States,

is preserved by the States, and may be destroyed by the States; and yet we are told that it is not a Government of the States."

And that, of course, was the crux of the matter. But much of this bluster about nationalism and sectionalism, federal power and states' rights, was a way to avoid talking more about the actual, brutal matters at hand: the conquest of lands held for ages by indigenous peoples and the existence of people within the United States who were denied every possible protection offered by a nation-state or, for that matter, a state-nation, people held as property.

Inevitably, the age of national bootblacks and national oyster houses and national blacksmiths produced national history books. The first major history of the American nation, George Bancroft's epic ten-volume *History of the United States from the Discovery of the American Continent to the Present*, was published between 1834 and 1874. Bancroft served in the administrations of three U.S. presidents, including as secretary of the navy during the age of American expansion. He celebrated American democracy, the first democracy in the modern world, and also promoted the idea of "manifest destiny," Americans' sense of their God-given right to cross the continent, seizing lands occupied by indigenous peoples and claimed by European nations from Russia to Spain to France. He wrote a history that tried to turn the state into a nation. To that end, he attempted to make America's founding appear inevitable and its growth inexorable. He wanted to give a very young country an ancient past. That's why he started not in 1776, when the United States declared its independence, which, arguably, is when anything properly called the "history of the United States" in fact begins, but in 1492, with "the Discovery of the Continent." Bancroft wanted the nation to appear older to give it more dignity and more authority and also, simply, more history.

Early national histories always worked this way. Everyone has to push a cart uphill. What changes, from one nation to another, is the angle of incline and the length of the slope. The "French nation" was an invention, and to make it seem less so the French had to acquire an ancient past, one that erased or ignored all other distinctions. Normans, Alsatians, Protestants, Basques, Parisians, Jews, Muslims—everyone within the boundaries of the state of France, no matter how they thought of themselves or what languages they spoke or what gods they worshipped—were to now see themselves as "French" and, still more strangely, to believe that they always had been. Having created Italy, it was now necessary to make Italians, said the nineteenth-century statesman Massimo d'Azeglio. Most Hungarians only found out that their nation had gotten its start in the year 896 ten centuries later. European immigrants to the United States often only learned that they belonged to a particular nation when they were asked to list a "nationality" on immigration forms.

The nationalism that George Bancroft set about cultivating in his *History of the United States* was part of this larger nineteenth-century project of sorting the world's peoples into nationalities. Like Jedidiah Morse's geography books and Noah Webster's spelling books, Bancroft's history aimed to promote a feeling of national attachment in a remarkably fast-changing U.S. population, a population that experienced a rate of growth never before known in the history of the world, a population overwhelmingly made up of immigrants and the children of immigrants.

The United States was founded as an asylum and a refuge: a sanctuary. This was a form of patriotism. Thomas Paine in *Common Sense* called America "an asylum for mankind." The Declaration of Inde-

pendence cites, as one of the abuses of the king, his
having discouraged and even prevented people from
coming into the colonies by "obstructing the Laws for
Naturalization" and "refusing to pass others to encour-
age their migrations hither." "I had always hoped that
this land might become a safe & agreeable Asylum to
the virtuous & persecuted part of mankind, to whatever nation they might belong," George Washington
wrote in 1788. Thomas Jefferson in 1817 described
the United States as offering "a sanctuary for those
whom the misrule of Europe may compel to seek happiness in other climes." The idea of the United States
as a sanctuary both mitigated American nationalism
and strengthened Americans' commitment to universalism. "We love our country, but not blindly," the
Unitarian minister William Ellery Channing proclaimed in 1823. "In all nations we recognize one
great family." "Nationality is a good thing to a certain
extent," Henry Wadsworth Longfellow wrote in 1849,
"but universality is better." Or, as Oliver Wendell
Holmes would write in 1858, "We are the Romans
of the modern world—the great assimilating people."
It was this tradition on which Barack Obama drew,
introducing himself to the American people in 2008.
"I am the son of a black man from Kenya and a white

woman from Kansas," he said. "These people are a part of me. And they are part of America." Obama's American family—Obama's America—was black and white and brown, and came from all over the world. "I have brothers, sisters, nieces, nephews, uncles and cousins, of every race and every hue, scattered across three continents, and for as long as I live, I will never forget that in no other country on Earth is my story even possible."

Obama, of course, didn't invent this idea, a civic and constitutional patriotism, however much his election realized its promise and his eloquence elevated it. The first part of Bancroft's *History of the United States* is the story of the English people planting a new nation. But Bancroft also celebrated the United States as a pluralist and cosmopolitan nation whose history was that of a people descended not from a shared set of ancestors but from all the cultures of the world. "France contributed to its independence," he observed, "the origin of the language we speak carries us to India; our religion is from Palestine; of the hymns sung in our churches, some were first heard in Italy, some in the deserts of Arabia, some on the banks of the Euphrates; our arts come from Greece; our jurisprudence from Rome."

To love this particular nation is to love the world. This paradox lies within all forms of liberal nationalism. A liberal nation is a nation to which anyone who affirms its civic ideals belongs.

· V ·

LIBERALISM AND NATIONALISM

Liberalism is the belief that people are good and should be free, and that people erect governments in order to guarantee that freedom. Nineteenth-century nationalism and modern liberalism were formed out of the same clay. Nations are collectives and liberalism concerns individuals; liberal nations are collections of individuals whose rights as citizens are guaranteed by the nation. Liberal governments require a popular mandate to rule: liberal nations are self-governed. Their rise marked the end of monarchical rule. *L'état, c'est moi,* Louis XIV is said to have proclaimed, but as his great-grandson Louis XV is said to have exclaimed, when he first heard the word "nation," "Nation! What is Nation? Is there anything beside myself?" With the rise of liberal nation-states, the state became the people: it required their consent. *L'état, c'est nous.*

But if formed out of the same clay, nationalism and liberalism were molded into different shapes. Liberalism embraced a set of aspirations about liberty and democracy believed to be universal. Bancroft went so far as to trace them back in time to all corners of the globe. But nationalism promotes attachment to a particular place, by insisting on national distinctions. How can a set of ideas believed to be universal undergird a national identity? Only if the people who subscribe to that set of ideas believe that, sooner or later, they will be everywhere adopted.

In the meantime, all sorts of people were left out of American nationalism's seeming universalism, just as they were excluded from citizenship in the nation. For most of American history, the vast majority of the world's peoples were ineligible for U.S. citizenship due to their race, origin, or sex. The Naturalization Act of 1790 offered naturalization only to "free white persons." And Bancroft, after all, wrote the history of the United States as the history of the providential founding of the world's first modern democracy by the "white man," after his conquest over "savages."

Bancroft believed that slavery was a national sin and warned that it would doom the Republic; he blamed Africans: "negro slavery is not an invention of the white man." Bancroft's universalism was no universalism at all.

A nation that declares most of the peoples of the world ineligible for citizenship and yet also describes itself as an asylum is defined by contradiction. But the United States, rebuked by all those left out of its vision of the nation, began battling that contradiction early on, and has never stopped. In the United States, the nation *is* that battle.

Many nineteenth-century Americans, themselves immigrants and the children and grandchildren of immigrants, considered other people who came to the United States to be forever foreigners. Fourteen-year-old Afong Moy, who arrived in New York from China in 1834, was exhibited as a curiosity—gawkers paid fifty cents to see her, with her tiny, bound feet, and wearing her "national costume." She toured the country, eventually with P. T. Barnum, as part of a collection of "nationalities." Then, too, some people in the United States, and in other nations as well, wanted no part of joining a nationality. They'd heard that they were supposed to think of themselves as "French" or

"German" or "American"—and they refused. This distressed advocates of liberal nationalism. "It is in general a necessary condition of free institutions, that the boundaries of government should coincide in the main with those of nationalities," wrote John Stuart Mill in 1861. Mill could not fathom how anyone living in France, of whatever ethnic or regional or linguistic or religious minority, could object to the idea of belonging to the French nation, when citizenship in a liberal nation brought so many benefits. "Nobody can suppose that it is not more beneficial to a Breton, or a Basque of French Navarre, to be . . . a member of the French nationality, admitted on equal terms to all the privileges of French citizenship, sharing the advantages of French protection and the dignity and prestige of French power," said Mill, "than to sulk on his own rocks, the half-savage relic of past times, revolving in his own little mental orbit, without participation or interest in the general movement of the world." This was Mill's blind spot.

The generation of mid-nineteenth-century intellectuals who advanced the idea of liberal nationalism were baffled by people like Basque separatists because liberal nationalists saw becoming a nation and belonging to a nationality as necessary and even inevitable steps on a path of moral, social, and political progress. Liberal nationalism, as an idea, is fundamentally historical. The case for the nation, in the nineteenth century, was less that the nation was a natural category than that the nation was a historical development. Liberal nationalism rested on an analogy between the individual and the collective. Just as liberals had faith in individuals, so they had faith in nations. That faith rested on the idea that the equal rights of individuals can *only* be guaranteed by their becoming the citizens of nations: that's what hitched liberalism to nationalism. No nations, no constitutions; no constitutions, no citizens; no citizens, no rights.

By the middle of the nineteenth century, liberalism and nationalism were as intricately intertwined in American politics as they were in the affairs of Europe. Abraham Lincoln described himself as "no less than National in all the positions I may take," by which he meant that he was not a sectionalist. But he also drew the liberal nationalist's analogy between the citizen and the nation. "My faith in the proposition that each man should do precisely as he pleases with all which is exclusively his own, lies at the foundation of the sense of justice there is in me. I extend the principles to communities of men, as well as to individuals."

Still, the relationship between liberalism and nationalism was also different in the United States than in Europe, because the United States had gotten its start as a state-nation, instead of a nation-state; because Americans understood their nation as an asylum; and because Americans who had been left out of the founding rejected the idea of the nation as progress. The United States had its own Basques. They answered American nationalism with denunciation, and by inventing their own.

· VI ·

NATIONS AND CITIZENS

A nation founded on the idea that all men are created equal and endowed with inalienable rights and offering asylum to anyone suffering from persecution is a beacon to the world. This is America at its best: a nation that welcomes dissent, protects free speech, nurtures invention, and makes possible almost unbelievable growth and prosperity. But a nation founded on ideals, universal truths, also opens itself to charges of hypocrisy at every turn. Those charges do not lie outside the plot of the story of America, or underneath it. They are its plot, the history on which any twenty-first-century case for the American nation has to rest, a history of struggle and agony and courage and promise.

It begins with fury. In 1833, William Apess, a Pequot minister from New England, wrote an essay called "An Indian's Looking-Glass for the White Man." He began by pointing out that, worldwide, white people were vastly outnumbered by "colored people": "Assemble all nations together in your imagination, and then let the whites be seated among them, and then let us look for the whites, and I doubt not it would be hard finding them: for to the rest of the nations, they are still but a handful," Apess wrote. He then proposed a thought experiment. "Now suppose these skins were put together, and each skin had its national crimes written upon it—which skin do you think would have the greatest? I will ask one question more. Can you charge the Indians with robbing a nation almost of their whole Continent, and murdering their women and children, and then depriving the remainder of their lawful rights, that nature and God require them to have?" Also, looking to the question of African slavery, he wondered what other nation in the world was guilty of stealing the people of another nation "to till their grounds, and welter out their days under the lash with hunger and fatigue." Yet for all the fury of his indictment, Apess ended his essay with a patriotic plea for the United States, praying that "the mantle of prejudice" would be "torn from every American heart—then shall peace pervade the Union."

Apess is a good illustration of an observation made by the political historian Michael Kazin, that it's nearly impossible to name "any American radical or reformer who repudiated the national belief system and still had a major impact on U.S. politics and policy." Patriotism, Kazin pointed out, has been indispensable to the Left, from Elizabeth Cady Stanton to Eugene Debs to Martin Luther King Jr.: "Americans who want to transform the world have to learn how to persuade the nation."

Apess wrote "An Indian's Looking-Glass for the White Man" just when Bancroft began writing his *History of the United States*, during Andrew Jackson's campaign of "Indian Removal." Under Jackson's policy, the federal government forced native peoples living east of the Mississippi, including the Choctaws, Creeks, Seminoles, and Chickasaws, to lands to the west, a policy that reached its greatest fury with the forced march of the Cherokee in what came to be called the Trail of Tears. It was said of Bancroft's *History* that it "voted for Jackson" on every page. As both men saw it, the indigenous peoples of the Americas were destined to yield their land to the peoples of Europe. Native peoples fought against Jackson's policy, with arms, and they also fought it through assertions of their own nationhood.

The Cherokee, who had acted as a nation in making treaties with the United States in 1785, 1791, and 1817, adopted their own Constitution, describing the Cherokee people as having "become one body politic, under the style and title of the Cherokee Nation." Defying the jurisdiction of the state of Georgia, they brought their battle for recognition to the national government, the U.S. Supreme Court, which ruled native peoples "domestic dependent nations." This status derived from a long recognition of native peoples as "nations," sovereign peoples capable of making treaties with other nations. As the Supreme Court ruled, "The very term 'nation,' so generally applied to them, means 'a people distinct from others.'"

In the centuries since, nearly six hundred native nations have been recognized by the U.S. government. Some native nations have also sought recognition from international authorities. Levi General, known as Deskaheh, in 1923 traveled through Europe on an Iroquois passport with the hope of addressing the League of Nations. Mohawk ironworker Paul Diabo in the 1920s crossed the border from Canada to the United States without a U.S. passport, later citing in court his right to travel unrestricted under the 1794 Jay Treaty. In the 1970s, the native peoples of Canada began calling themselves the "First Nations," and in the United States, both the American Indian Movement and the National Congress of American Indians called for sovereignty through nationhood. In 2010, the Iroquois Nation's lacrosse team tried to use Iroquois passports to enter the UK for a world championship tournament. In 2016, the Standing Rock Sioux and thousands of other native peoples from the historical Great Sioux Nation and beyond, along with their allies, protested the Dakota Access pipeline, a battle they took to federal courts and to the United Nations Human Rights Council.

Challenges like the struggle for native nationhood constitute the American nation in much the same way that the debates over the Constitution constitute the nation. They challenge the nation to live up to its ideals. So have centuries-long struggles for emancipation and civil rights. In 1829, David Walker, a free black man, published *An Appeal to the Coloured Citizens of the World, but in Particular, and Very Expressly, to those of the United States of America*. Calling slavery a "curse to nations" and citing the Declaration of Independence, Walker demanded that the United States abolish slavery and honor its obligations to citizens of all colors, asking of "the American people themselves" to show him a truly equal colored citizen: "Not, indeed, to show me a coloured President, a Governor, a Legislator, a Senator, a Mayor, or an Attorney at the Bar.—But to show me a man of colour, who holds the low office of a Constable, or one who sits in a Juror Box, even on a case of one of his wretched brethren, throughout this great Republic!!" And yet Walker, like Apess, ended his indictment not with damnation but with a plea for a better America, a new Americanism. "Treat us then like men," he said. "And there is not a doubt in my mind, but that the whole of the past will be sunk into oblivion, and we yet, under God, will become a united and happy people."

Nations have historically been figured as brotherhoods—*"treat us then like men."* If the nation was a family, only fathers and sons were citizens. Women, and girls, as future women, were "the mothers of nations," cherished for reproducing the nation by bearing sons. But in 1831, Maria W. Stewart, a free black woman in Boston, carried Walker's argument further: *treat us then like men—and women.* "How long shall the fair daughters of Africa be compelled to bury their minds and talents beneath a load of iron pots and kettles?" she demanded. "I am a true born American," she told an audience. *"Your* blood flows in *my* veins, and your spirit fires my breast." White women demanded their rights as citizens, too. At the first women's rights convention, in Seneca Falls, New York, in 1848, Elizabeth Cady Stanton drafted a Declaration of Sentiments, a patriotic appeal to the Declaration of Independence: "in view of this entire disfranchisement of one-half the people of this country," she wrote, "we insist that they have immediate admission to all the rights and privileges which belong to them as citizens of these United States."

It would take a very long time for the United States to answer these charges and meet these demands. It has yet to answer and meet them all. But its commitment to the freedoms of speech and press and assembly—its commitment to a rights-based liberalism—made these and other political claims possible. "The great glory of American democracy is the right to protest for right," as Martin Luther King Jr. once said.

The nation is often wrong. But so long as protest is possible, it can always be righted.

· VII ·

NATIONS AND PROGRESS

"We bear the ark of the liberties of the world," Herman Melville wrote in 1850, conjuring an American nationalism that would be handed down across the generations as both a set of aspirations for self-government and a manifesto for imperialism. Melville's nationalism was the product of an era marked by nativism. In the 1840s, Americans opposed to a new wave of immigrants, chiefly Irish and German Catholics, founded a new political party, the Native American Party, also known as the American Party, or the Know-Nothings. "The grand work of the American party," they said, "is the principle of nationality."

This principle was also used to justify wars against native peoples in the West and, in 1846, against Mexico. "The late conquest of Mexico found us not wanting in the sentimentality of *nationalism*," wrote one observer. But American nationalism cut the other way, too. Many were those who protested Indian removal, slavery, and the war with Mexico, on the grounds that these things broke faith with American ideals. "Abroad we are looked on as a nation of swindlers and menstealers!" the Unitarian minister Theodore Parker lamented in 1846. "Alas, the nation is a traitor to its great idea—that all men are born equal, each with the same inalienable rights." Abraham Lincoln rejected the message of President James Polk, damning Polk's call for war with Mexico in the name of "national honor" as "the half insane mumbling of a fever-dream." Said Henry David Thoreau, who went to jail rather than pay taxes to contribute to the war, "I quietly declare war with the State."

Frederick Douglass, who had also protested the war with Mexico, declared his own war with the state. Invited in 1852 to deliver an oration on Independence Day, he told his white audience, "This Fourth of July

is yours, not mine. You may rejoice, I must mourn. . . .
Fellow-citizens; above your national, tumultuous joy,
I hear the mournful wail of millions!" In that wail,
Douglass founded his own political claim. "There is
not a man beneath the canopy of heaven, that does not
know that slavery is wrong for him," he said, calling
for a new founding for the nation, on the toppled ruins
of its past hypocrisy. And yet, even in his despair, and
within his very indictment of that spectacle of patriotism, the Fourth of July, Douglass expressed a love
of country, too, finding hope in and "encouragement
from the Declaration of Independence, the great principles it contains, and the genius of American Institutions," whose commitments he challenged his fellow
Americans to honor.

The case for the nation in the twenty-first century
rests on the writings of each of these Americans as
much as it rests on the force and eloquence of the
framers of the Constitution. Their arguments about
the nation developed within, and advanced, an emerg-
ing set of ideas about human rights: the power of the
state guaranteed all those eligible for citizenship the
same set of political rights, equal and irrevocable,
no matter their color, religion, or nation of birth. In
1849 the Massachusetts abolitionist and later sen-

ator Charles Sumner invoked this set of ideas when he described the constitution of his home state: "Here is the Great Charter of every human being drawing vital breath upon this soil, whatever may be his condition, and whoever may be his parents. He may be poor, weak, humble, or black,—he may be of Caucasian, Jewish, Indian, or Ethiopian race,—he may be of French, German, English, or Irish extraction; but before the Constitution of Massachusetts all these distinctions disappear. . . . He is a Man, the equal of all his fellow-men. He is one of the children of the State, which, like an impartial parent, regards all its offspring with an equal care."

But the charter of liberty was meaningless in states that countenanced slavery, as critics both within and outside the United States had long charged. Slavery impeded the progress promised by nationhood. Lincoln made this argument plain before an audience in Peoria, Illinois, in 1854:

> *Fellow countrymen— . . . the liberal party throughout the world, express the apprehension "that the one retrograde institution in America, is undermining the principles of progress, and fatally violating the noblest political system the world ever saw."*

*This is not the taunt of enemies, but the warning
of friends. Is it quite safe to disregard it—to despise
it? Is there no danger to liberty itself, in discard-
ing the earliest practice, and first precept of our
ancient faith? In our greedy chase to make profit
of the negro, let us beware, lest we "cancel and tear
to pieces" even the white man's charter of freedom.*

Lincoln begged his audience to address slavery, for
the sake of the nation. "If we do this, we shall not only
have saved the Union; but we shall have so saved it, as
to make, and to keep it, forever worthy of the saving.
We shall have so saved it, that the succeeding millions of free happy people, the world over, shall rise
up, and call us blessed, to the latest generations."

If liberal progress, the progress of freedom, only
takes place through the formation of nations, which
alone can guarantee that freedom, the dissolution of
the Union meant a step backward. "The present period
will be called the National Period," wrote Prussian-
born American political philosopher Franz Lieber, in
an influential essay called "Nationalism: A Fragment
of Political Science," in which he explained the relationship between the nation and progress. "No group-
ings of human beings, short of nations, are adequate

to the high demands of modern civilization," Lieber wrote from New York. "Without a national character, States cannot obtain that longevity and continuity of political society which is necessary for our progress."

But "Nationalism: A Fragment of Political Science" appeared in 1860, on the very eve of the Civil War. The next year, the American charter was torn to fragments.

· VIII ·

TWO NATIONALISMS

The American Civil War was a struggle between two nationalisms. In the antebellum United States, Northerners and especially Northern abolitionists drew a contrast between (Northern) nationalism and (Southern) sectionalism. "We must cultivate a *national*, instead of a *sectional* patriotism," urged one Michigan congressman in 1850. But Southerners were nationalists, too. It's just that their nationalism, at the time, was what would now be termed illiberal, or ethnic, as against another liberal, or civic, nationalism.

Since about the middle of the twentieth century, people who've wanted to wrest the word "nationalism" away from the bloody hands of tyrants have tried to distinguish between "good nationalism" and "bad nationalism." By good nationalism, they usually mean liberal or civic nationalism, an attachment to a set of civic ideals. By bad nationalism, they usually mean illiberal or ethnic nationalism, nativism, racism, and recourse to aggression. American nationalism is often figured as one or the other, but really it's almost always been both.

"Ours is the Government of the white man," South Carolina's John C. Calhoun declared in 1848, arguing against admitting as citizens of the United States the people of Mexico, people he did not consider to be white. "I protest against the incorporation of such a people," Calhoun said. Calhoun's was a race-based nationalism: the United States was to be a white nation. This view was not confined to the South. Oregon in 1857 adopted something close to a whites-only constitution: "No negro, Chinaman, or mulatto shall have the right of suffrage," it declared. That same year, in *Dred Scott v. Sandford*, the U.S. Supreme Court ruled that no person of African descent could ever become a citizen of the United States, on the grounds that the framers of the Constitution had viewed Africans as "beings of an inferior order, and altogether unfit to associate with the white race, either in social or political relations; and so far inferior, that they had no rights which the white man was bound to respect." (The court also ruled, in *Dred Scott*, that Native Americans were not similarly barred from ever becoming naturalized citizens of the United States; instead, they were perfectly eligible, like people from any other foreign nations, to become U.S. citizens.)

An American nationalism descended from these illiberal traditions endures, a scourge to the country and the world. But out of the fiery trial of argument and, finally, of war, a liberal nationalism endured, too.

"This Government was made by our fathers on the white basis," Illinois senator and onetime judge Stephen Douglas said in 1858. "It was made by white men for the benefit of white men and their posterity forever." It fell to Abraham Lincoln to counter this argument, exposing Douglas's history as fiction: "I believe the entire records of the world, from the date of the Declaration of Independence up to within three years ago, may be searched in vain for one single affirmation, from one single man, that the negro was not included in the Declaration of Independence;

I think I may defy Judge Douglas to show that he ever said so, that Washington ever said so, that any President ever said so, that any member of Congress ever said so, or that any living man upon the whole earth ever said so, until the necessities of the present policy of the Democratic party, in regard to slavery, had to invent that affirmation."

No matter, the founders of the Confederacy answered: we will craft a new constitution. In 1861, the Confederacy's newly elected vice president, Alexander Stephens, delivered a speech in Savannah in which he explained that the ideas that lay behind the Constitution of the United States "rested upon the assumption of the equality of races"—here ceding Lincoln's argument—but "Our new Government is founded upon exactly the opposite idea; its foundations are laid, its cornerstone rests, upon the great truth that the negro is not equal to the white man; that slavery, subordination to the superior race, is his natural and moral condition. This, our new Government, is the first, in the history of the world, based upon this great physical, philosophical, and moral truth."

Native peoples rejected both of these nationalisms. They allied with both sides during the war, and for many, the U.S. Civil War was nothing so much as a continuation of earlier wars. The Union army killed massive numbers of Indians during the war, including at Sand Creek and Bear River, on the Navajo Long Walk, and during the Dakota Uprising reprisals. Those Indians who sided with the Confederacy did so not out of loyalty to the Southern states but out of disaffection with the federal government, which had announced a plan to seize and open to white settlement lands to the west of the Mississippi known as the Indian Territory. The Confederacy sought and succeeded in securing alliances with Comanches, Chickasaws, Choctaws, Seminoles, and Creeks who, in effect, seceded along with the Confederate states.

To the Union, and to the Confederacy, Lincoln used the power of his voice to make the case for the nation. At Gettysburg in 1863, he prayed that "this nation, under God, shall have a new birth of freedom—and that government of the people, by the people, for the people, shall not perish from the earth." He would die for this vision of the nation, and of citizenship. On April 11, 1865, two days after Lee surrendered to Grant, John Wilkes Booth saw Lincoln deliver a speech about the terms of the victory. "That means nigger citizenship," Booth seethed. On April 14, he shot Lincoln in Ford's Theatre. The

nation went into mourning. Among the thousands
of heartfelt tributes and prayers was one offered at
a meeting of the Mexican Patriotic Club on April
23, in Virginia City, Nevada, by Mexican Americans
who remembered Lincoln's opposition to the war
with Mexico. "Mejicanos!" Rafael Gonzalez shouted.
"Llorémos la pérdida de este virtuoso ciudadano,
mártir de la libertad de América: Sí llorémosle,
porque ha sido víctima de un asesinato. Mas sus doc-
trinas que entraño en el corazon de los pueblos no
desaparecerán jamás, y su nombre será eternizado
en la historia." (Mexicans! Let us cry for the loss of
this virtuous citizen, martyr for the liberty of America: Let us cry, because he has been the victim of an
assassination. His teachings, deep within the heart
of the people, shall never disappear, and his name
shall live forever in history.)

Lincoln was not forgotten. Nor was the fight
between federal power and states' rights. "Are We a
Nation?" Charles Sumner asked in 1867, damning
states' rights as "denationalizing." This, of course, did
not settle the question. And, after the war, the battle between Americans' two nationalisms would be
fought, all over again, in new battles over citizenship
and sovereignty and rights, and immigration.

· IX ·

A NEW NATION

During the Civil War, the idea of the American nation had been bloodied in battle, chastened by its critics, and uplifted by Lincoln. After the war, the Fourteenth and Fifteenth Amendments founded the United States all over again, on terms set by liberal ideas about the rights of citizens and the powers of nation-states.

The Fourteenth Amendment, adopted in 1868, established birthright citizenship: "All persons born or naturalized in the United States, and subject to the jurisdiction thereof, are citizens of the United States and of the State wherein they reside." It guaranteed citizens equal rights: "No state shall make or enforce any law which shall abridge the privileges or immunities of citizens of the United States." And it provided protections to noncitizens: "nor shall any state deprive any person of life, liberty, or property, without due process of law; nor deny to any person within its jurisdiction the equal protection of the laws."

The Fifteenth Amendment, adopted in 1870, was

meant to prevent states from depriving citizens of their suffrages, in any state: "the right of citizens of the United States to vote shall not be denied or abridged by the United States or by any State on account of race, color, or previous condition of servitude."

As had happened in the 1840s during the debate over the annexation of territories acquired from Mexico, the debates over the drafting and ratification of these amendments involved an attempt to settle questions about immigration, equality, and citizenship. These questions involved not only people of African descent but also people of Asian descent. In the 1850s, Chinese men, mostly from the southern Chinese province of Guangdong, had begun arriving in large numbers, especially in San Francisco, and settling all over the West, where they most often worked as miners, or on railroads. "Americans are very rich people," read ads recruiting migrants, largely through *gam saan jong*, or Gold Mountain firms. "They want the Chinaman to come." In the United States, they found employment but little more. Nine out of ten men building the Pacific Central Railroad were Chinese, but when as many as five thousand of them went on strike in 1867, complaining, "Eight hours a day good for white men, all the same good for Chinamen," they were starved into abandoning the protest.

An 1868 treaty between China and the United States suggested that Chinese immigrants be treated like citizens, but it afforded them no actual protection. Under the terms of the Fourteenth Amendment's birthright citizenship clause, any children who were born to Chinese immigrants in the United States would be American citizens, by right of birth, a right consistent with a liberal view of citizenship. Lyman Trumbull, a senator from Illinois, insisted, "the child of an Asiatic is just as much a citizen as the child of a European." But Trumbull, who had helped to draft the Thirteenth Amendment, which abolished slavery, was one of only a very small number of men in Congress who talked about Chinese immigrants in favorable terms, describing them as "citizens from that country which in many respects excels any other country on the face of the globe in the arts and sciences, among whose population are to be found the most learned and eminent scholars in the world." William Higby, a Republican congressman from California and a one-time miner, vented a more commonly held view. "The Chinese are nothing but a pagan race," he said. "You cannot make good citizens of them."

The Fifteenth Amendment, proposed early in 1869, aimed to guarantee African Americans the right to vote and hold office, but its language again raised the question of Chinese citizenship and suffrage. Opponents of the amendment found its entire premise outrageous. Garrett Davis, a Democratic senator from Kentucky, insisted, "I want no negro government; I want no Mongolian government; I want the government of the white man which our fathers incorporated." Hoping to secure passage, Michigan's Jacob Howard suggested that the Fifteenth Amendment specifically bar Chinese men and apply only to "citizens of the United States of African descent." Howard seems to have been acting on the assumption that Chinese exclusion would improve the chances of the amendment's passage and ratification. But congressional enthusiasm for immigration thwarted his proposal. George F. Edmunds of Vermont called Howard's revision to the amendment an outrage, pointing out that it would enfranchise black men only by leaving out "the native of every other country under the sun."

The most important address of this era was the one that most expansively expressed the ideas of liberal nationalism: Frederick Douglass's "Composite Nation." In 1869, Douglass delivered this speech to

audiences all over the country, celebrating the Fourteenth and Fifteenth Amendments as necessary to
what he called, in language not yet widely adopted,
"human rights." He began by speaking, he said, "to the
question whether we are the better or the worse for
being composed of different races of men." If nations,
which are essential for progress, form from similar-
ity, what of nations like the United States, which are
formed from difference? Douglass located the origins
of the struggle over American national identity not
in the founding documents but in the people themselves. "The real trouble with us was never our system
or form of Government, or the principles underlying
it; but the peculiar composition of our people," he
said. Americans, he said, are "the most conspicuous
example of composite nationality in the world." This
was not the nation's weakness but its strength.

Native American, African, and European, and
every possible mixture, the peoples of the United
States now confronted the question of immigration
from Asia, Douglass said. "Do you ask, if I favor such
immigration, I answer I would. Would you have them
naturalized, and have them invested with all the
rights of American citizenship? I would. Would you
allow them to vote? I would. Would you allow them to

hold office? I would." Why? Because "there are such things in the world as human rights," he answered, and "when there is a supposed conflict between human and national rights, it is safe to go to the side of humanity."

No one of his generation stated the case more squarely. As for future generations, Douglass went on, "I want a home here not only for the negro, the mulatto and the Latin races; but I want the Asiatic to find a home here in the United States, and feel at home here, both for his sake and for ours. Right wrongs no man."

For Douglass, the greatest progress could be realized only in a very particular kind of nation, the composite nation—that asylum, refuge, and sanctuary—a home for "all who seek their shelter whether from Asia, Africa, or the Isles of the sea," a nation of civic ideals where "all shall here bow to the same law, speak the same language, support the same Government, enjoy the same liberty, vibrate with the same national enthusiasm, and seek the same national ends."

Emancipation and Reconstruction, W. E. B. DuBois would write, had been "the finest effort to achieve democracy . . . this world had ever seen." That effort was betrayed after the end of Reconstruction by white

Northerners and white Southerners who patched the country back together by inventing a myth that the war hadn't been fought over slavery at all; instead, it had been a struggle between the nation and the states. "We fell under the leadership of those who would compromise with truth in the past in order to make peace in the present," DuBois wrote bitterly.

DuBois's reckoning with American history was, for a very long time, ignored. And Frederick Douglass's Americanism did not then prevail. But they're still there, traditions waiting to be claimed, challenges waiting to be met.

· X ·

RACE AND NATION

"Nations are something rather new in history," the French philosopher Ernest Renan observed in 1882, in a widely read essay called "What Is a Nation?" "Nations are not eternal," he went on. "They have a beginning and they will have an end." Meanwhile, "the existence of nations is a good and even necessary thing," and so it was worth his asking: What even are they? On what basis are they formed? What holds them together? Not a unity of religion or language and most definitely not the pseudoscience of race; if that were so, Renan wrote, "The limits of states would thus follow the fluctuations of scientific knowledge and patriotism would depend on a more or less paradoxical dissertation. One would come to say to the patriot: 'You were wrong. You spilled your blood for this cause, believing that you were a Celt. No, you are a German.' Then, ten years later, one would discover that you are in fact a Slav." And what of a shared past? Only insofar as it is a fiction. Getting its history wrong is part of being a nation, Renan concluded: "Forgetting, I would even say historical error, is an essential factor in the creation of a nation and it is for this reason that the progress of historical studies often poses a threat to nationality."

Two years later, the American Historical Association was founded. Historical inquiry, in the United States and in Europe, was becoming a profession at the very moment when nationalism was taking a turn away from liberalism and toward illiberalism, beginning in Germany with the "blood and iron" of Otto von Bismarck. Bismarck, as minister-president of Prussia,

led wars against Denmark, Austria, and France; organized North Germany into a federation in 1867; and
established the German Empire in 1871, with himself
as chancellor. He waged a campaign to reunify Germany in the name of a Germanic "race," while pursu-
ing a policy of "Germanization" of minorities.

Illiberal nationalism is often thought of as what
happens when a nation-state demands extraordinary
sacrifices from its people—especially by participation in wars of aggression—and, requiring their consent, asks for that sacrifice in the name of the nation.
The more outrageous the war, the harder it is to gain
that consent, the more grotesque the depiction of the
nation's enemies.

But illiberal nationalism is an outgrowth of other
late nineteenth-century developments as well, including mass politics, mass communication, and mass
migration. More than twenty million Europeans emigrated to the United States between 1880 and 1920.
The smaller and more fluid the world became, the
flimsier were stories of ancient nations made of a single people, united by a shared line of descent, and the
more eagerly people keen for political power searched
for rationales for exclusion, discrimination, and
aggression. New racial "sciences," above all the quack-

ery of eugenics, purported to cull the worthy from the unworthy; sorting out peoples into "nationalities" very soon meant sorting them out by "races," to be ranked hierarchically.

In 1882, the year Ernest Renan asked "What Is a Nation?," the United States passed its first major law restricting immigration, the Chinese Exclusion Act. "Every nation has the right to refuse to admit a foreigner into the country," the legal theorist Emer de Vattel had written in 1758, in *The Law of Nations*. The logic behind this idea had been that foreigners might be agents of an enemy nation. But what about immigrants from nations that were not enemies? In 1889 the Supreme Court ruled that they, too, could be barred, decreeing that if Congress "considers the presence of foreigners of a different race in this country, who will not assimilate with us, to be dangerous to its peace and security, their exclusion is not to be stayed because at the time there are no actual hostilities with the nation of which the foreigners are subject."

To restrict immigration, a practice associated with the rise of illiberal nationalism, is to regard foreigners who arrive from friendly nations as invading armies. In the United States, founded as an asylum for the oppressed, this was a very hard turn. Creating a justification for it led to the embrace of eugenics; a newly focused anti-Semitism; and fearmongering about Catholicism and socialism as European imports, the one seen as just this side of monarchism, the other just this side of anarchism. The American Protective Association, an anti-Catholic secret society founded in 1887, carried on the tradition of the Know-Nothing Party. In 1888, the American Economic Association offered a prize for the best essay on "The Evil Effects of Unrestricted Immigration." By 1894, three Harvard alumni had founded the Immigration Restriction League, based in Boston. But the growth of illiberal nationalism was also very closely tied to the growth of populism, especially in the Midwest and West, as white farmers and wage laborers left behind in the Gilded Age's economy looked for explanations for their suffering, and searched for enemies.

In the United States, the race-based nationalism of the 1880s led to three sweeping policy changes: the rise of Jim Crow laws, instituting a regime of racial segregation that would be upheld by the Supreme Court in *Plessy v. Ferguson* in 1896; the passage of the Chinese Exclusion Act, prohibiting Chinese immigration and understood to restrict birthright citizenship;

and the Supreme Court's decision in *Elk v. Wilkins* in 1884, rejecting a citizenship claim by a Winnebago man named John Elk. In *Elk v. Wilkins* the court ruled that Fourteenth Amendment birthright citizenship did not apply to Native Americans, on the grounds that, born in a tribal community, Elk had not technically been "born in the United States"—leaving him, in the words of a dissenting opinion, "with no nationality whatsoever." Massachusetts senator Henry L. Dawes described *Elk v. Wilkins* as the "strangest, if not the wickedest decision since the fugitive slave cases."

Three years after *Elk v. Wilkins*, Congress passed the Dawes Act, granting citizenship to Native Americans who agreed to live apart from their people, in exchange for an allotment of land. The Dawes Act was meant to break up native communities. A "Citizenship Ritual" purported to turn native peoples "white" by the act of accepting a bow and arrow (for men), delivered with these words: "You have shot your last arrow. That means you are no longer to live the life of an Indian. You are from this day forward to live the life of the white man. But you may keep that arrow, it will be to you a symbol of your noble race and of the pride you feel that you come from the first of all Americans." Women were handed a work bag and purse and told, "This means that you have chosen the life of the white woman—and the white woman loves her home."

Segregation, exclusion, and the Dawes Act's quid pro quo citizenship betrayed the spirit, the liberal promises, and the constitutional guarantees of the Fourteenth and Fifteenth Amendments. But the very struggle to hold the nation to those promises would carry on a liberal tradition, one that cherished civic ideals and made claims for the nation.

In 1887, the same year Congress passed the Dawes Act, King Kalakaua of Hawai'i was all but forced to sign what came to be known as the Bayonet Constitution, under which Kanaka Maoli, or native Hawaiians, effectively ceded political power to white American settlers, in something of a prelude to U.S. annexation. After Kalakaua's death, in 1891, his sister Lili'uokalani defended the idea of Hawaiian nationhood, and proposed a new constitution, insisting on "the right of the Hawaiian people to choose their own form of government." She rejected the claims for political power of American missionaries and businessmen: "They are not and never were Hawaiians." And she cautioned against American imperialism: "Is the American Republic of States to degenerate, and become a colonizer and a land-grabber?"

If Queen Lili'uokalani did not stop annexation, or American imperial ventures in the Philippines and elsewhere, she established new terms for the debate. So did dissenters within the United States. "Why do they not legislate against Swedes, Germans, Italians, Turks and others?" asked Yung Hen, a Chinese poultry dealer in San Francisco in 1892. Wong Kim Ark, born in San Francisco in 1873 but refused reentry to the United States after a trip to China, took his case to the Supreme Court, which ruled in 1898 that, under the Fourteenth Amendment, birthright citizenship did indeed apply to Chinese Americans.

Fighting for the honoring of U.S. treaties and the guarantees of the Fourteenth and Fifteenth Amendments would be the ongoing work of generations of Americans, from indigenous rights organizations, to Italian, Jewish, and Slavic aid societies, like the Irish and German aid societies before them, to civil rights organizers, suffragists, feminists, and gay rights activists. They questioned the nature of a race-based nationalism and discrimination based on sex, gender, and sexuality. They resisted regimes of violence and reigns of terror. They started newspapers and magazines and founded voluntary associations. Ida B. Wells, born into slavery in Mississippi, led a national campaign against lynching and would go on, with W. E. B. DuBois, to help found the National Association for the Advancement of Colored People in 1909. In 1892, the year Wells published *Southern Horrors: Lynch Law in All Its Phases*, Wong Chin Foo, who'd earlier started the *Chinese American,* a New York city newspaper, founded the Chinese Equal Rights League, insisting, "We claim a common manhood with all other nationalities." A Jewish welfare worker named Nissim Behar founded the National Liberal Immigration League in 1906 to fight against immigration restriction. Two years later, and for the same purpose, Israel Zangwill, who helped run an emigration society for Russian Jews, called for a better Americanism in his play *The Melting-Pot.*

The demand that the United States realize the promise of its founding, and especially of its second founding, produced some of the most eloquent art and oratory in American history. In 1906, not many years after the nation's celebration of the four hundredth anniversary of Columbus's voyage, Chitto Harjo, from the Muscogee Creek Nation, delivered to a Senate committee meeting in Tulsa a history of the Creek people. "In 1492—there was a man by the name of

Columbus came from across the great ocean, and he discovered this country for the white man—this country which was at that time the home of my people." He chronicled removal in 1832, the Creek vantage on the Civil War—"I went in as a Union soldier"— and the betrayals after the war. "I am informed and believe it to be true that some citizens of the United States have titles to land that was given to my fathers and my people by the Government. If it was given to me, what right has the United States to take it from me without first asking my consent?"

The year that Chitto Harjo spoke to U.S. senators in Tulsa, Mary Church Terrell delivered a speech in Washington. In "What It Means to Be Colored in the Capital of the United States," Terrell, the Memphis-born daughter of former slaves, revisited the themes of Frederick Douglass's 1852 speech "What to the Slave Is the Fourth of July?"

As a colored woman I may walk from the Capitol to the White House, ravenously hungry and abundantly supplied with money with which to purchase a meal, without finding a single restaurant in which I would be permitted to take a morsel of food, if it was patronized by white people, unless

I were willing to sit behind a screen. As a colored
woman, I cannot visit the tomb of the Father of this
country, which owes its very existence to the love of
freedom in the human heart and which stands for
equal opportunity to all, without being forced to sit
in the Jim Crow section of an electric car. . . . If I
refuse thus to be humiliated, I am cast into jail.

Terrell demanded full citizenship. But women and
people of color also challenged American nationalism
by joining calls for internationalism. They pioneered
international organizations, finding common cause
with women and people of color in other countries.
Jamaican-born American Marcus Garvey founded the
Universal Negro Improvement Association in 1914
in Akron, Ohio, and four years later began printing
its official organ, *The Negro World*. Women explored
other ways of fighting for citizenship, or abdicating
it. "As a woman, I have no country," Virginia Woolf
would claim, echoing Karl Marx's insistence that
workers have no country. The International Council
of Women was founded at a meeting of the National
Woman Suffrage Association in 1888, Elizabeth Cady
Stanton remarking on a "universal sense of injustice,
that forms a common bond of union" among "the

women of all nationalities." By 1925, it claimed to have thirty-six million members. Black women, usually left out of white women's political organizations, or allowed to join but ignored—"The Colored women know that our group is much more skeptical about white women than the world knows anything about," said one—formed their own organizations, both national and international, from the National Association of Colored Women, founded in 1896, to the International Council of Women of the Darker Races, in 1920.

"Intersectional feminism," as it would come to be called decades later, has a long history. So does what might be thought of as intersectional Americanism. Asked to choose between being African and being American, or joining civil rights organizations, or feminist ones, a lot of people complained about the nature of the choice. Alice Woodby McKane, MD, expressed her support for Marcus Garvey's Universal Negro Improvement Association but rejected the idea that embracing Pan-Africanism constituted a conflict with her idea of Americanism. "I have also another racial blood in me, the American Indian, and that coupled with the fact that I was born here and that my ancestors both red and black have fought for all

that American Civilization holds dear, makes me feel
that no one has a better right to enjoy the rights and
privileges here than I and my kind."

These stories didn't make their way into early histories of the American nation. The nation's most deco-
rated historians—the men who delivered presidential
addresses at the annual meetings of the American
Historical Association during those years—had little
interest in protesting racial injustice, or forced assimilation, or female disenfranchisement, or immigration
restriction. More often, they favored these practices.
In "The Significance of the Frontier in American History" in 1893, Frederick Jackson Turner talked about
the frontier as a line between "savagery" and "civilization" where democracy was forged in violence. In
The Winning of the West (1889–1896), Theodore Roosevelt told the story of American history as the story
of white men's conquest over native peoples, four vol-
umes chronicling what he sometimes called "the great
epic feat in the history of our race." Woodrow Wilson, author of a five-volume *History of the American
People*, first published in 1902, died before he was
to deliver his presidential address before the AHA.
Throughout his life, he renounced sectionalism—"I
hold that a Government is what its people and its his-

tory make it and that our Government had been made national and indissoluble long before 1861"—even as he defended segregation, and oversaw the segregation of the civil service when he assumed the office of the president in 1913.

Progressive historians, most of all Charles Beard, explained American history as a story of economic conflict. Beard's sweeping and immensely popular textbooks, including the 1927 *Rise of American Civilization*, written with his wife, Mary Ritter Beard, offered a searching account of the origins of American democracy. The Beards' work, much beloved, called for and inspired patriotic sentiment. But they, too, left out from their account the very people who were still left out of the national community. As W. E. B. DuBois put it, one reads *The Rise of American Civilization* "with a comfortable feeling that nothing right or wrong is involved," as if evil were as authorless as weather.

DuBois, who earned his PhD at Harvard in 1895, was never elected president of the American Historical Association, but his histories have proved among the most durable of any written in this era. In *The Souls of Black Folk*, published in 1903, DuBois, introducing the idea of a double consciousness, reckoned with American history as a contest between competing kinds of belonging, to a race and to a nation. "The history of the American Negro is the history of this strife," DuBois wrote. "He would not Africanize America, for America has too much to teach the world and Africa. He would not bleach his Negro soul in a flood of white Americanism, for he knows that Negro blood has a message for the world. He simply wishes to make it possible for a man to be both a Negro and an American."

But the nation, eyeing both war and bolshevism in Europe, demanded an undivided loyalty. Theodore Roosevelt answered immigrants' attachments and DuBois's double consciousness with a demand for a single, national identity. "There is no room for the hyphen in our citizenship," Roosevelt said. "This is one of the demands to be made in the name of the spirit of American nationalism. The other is equally important. We must treat every good American of German descent or any other American, without regard to his creed, as on a full and exact equality with every other good American, and set our faces like flint against the creatures who seek to discriminate against such an American, or to hold against him the birthplace of himself or his parents." It was the first part of this speech (no hyphens), not the second part (no discrimination), that audiences remembered.

Roosevelt called for a "New Nationalism," beginning with a speech he delivered in 1910 in Osawatomie, Kansas, at the site of arguably the first battle of the nation's disunion, the 1856 fight between proslavery Kansans and abolitionists. "We are all Americans," Roosevelt said in Kansas. "The National Government belongs to the whole American people, and where the whole American people are interested, that interest can be guarded effectively only by the National Government."

Roosevelt's New Nationalism had been much influenced by Zangwill's 1908 *Melting-Pot*. "America is God's Crucible, the great Melting-Pot where all the races of Europe are melting and reforming!" Zangwill's hero says. "Germans and Frenchmen, Irishmen and Englishmen, Jews and Russians—into the Crucible with you all! God is making the American." Roosevelt wrote to Zangwill, "I do not know when I have seen a play that stirred me as much." But Roosevelt's New Nationalism, as both a slogan and a campaign, was borrowed from the Progressive journalist Herbert Croly. In 1908 Croly called for economic and social reform that would bring new immigrants more fully into national life. That call helped Roosevelt's New Nationalism attract social reformers, including Jane Addams and Lillian Wald, and proved central to the founding of the Progressive Party.

Roosevelt's nationalism was also a strange hybrid, at once liberal and illiberal. Roosevelt accepted the idea of black citizenship but wrote, privately, that there really was no solution to "the terrible problem offered by the presence of the negro on this continent." He saw the Spanish-American War as yet another battle in the national drama of racial conquest that he'd chronicled in *The Winning of the West.* He could imagine a melting pot for all Europeans, but for no one else. That dilemma lasted. But so did Woodby McKane's Americanism—"my ancestors both red and black have fought for all that American Civilization holds dear." She embraced what, beginning in 1915, was called "cultural pluralism," the idea that it was perfectly possible to identify as both American and something else, a position taken by the Jewish American philosopher Horace Kallen, who defined the United States as a "democracy of nationalities," a nation of nations.

And still the nation's two nationalisms battled one another. In 1912, Wilson defeated both Taft, the

Republican, and Roosevelt, the Progressive, and, three years later, in the White House, watched D. W. Griffith's pro-Confederacy film *The Birth of a Nation*, for which Griffith had relied, in part, on Wilson's *History of the American People*. Inspired by the film, the Ku Klux Klan, originally formed in the 1860s, was reborn in 1915 under the banner of "true Americanism." Its object was "to unite white male persons, native-born Gentile citizens of the United States . . . to maintain forever white supremacy" and to "conserve, protect and maintain the distinctive institutions, rights, privileges, principles, traditions and ideals of pure Americanism."

With terrifying strains of nationalism arising in Germany, and Klan membership growing in the United States, American nationalism in the first decades of the twentieth century also took the form of economic nationalism and advocacy of isolationism. Newspaper magnate William Randolph Hearst, opposing U.S. involvement in the war in Europe, printed editorials calling for "America First."

U.S. entry into the war only stoked nationalism. Wilson, in his Fourteen Points, argued for national self-determination, "the principle of justice to all peoples and nationalities, and their right to live on equal terms of liberty and safety with one another, whether they be strong or weak." But in 1919, at the close of the war, the U.S. Senate rejected the Treaty of Versailles, under whose terms the United States would join Wilson's long-sought international body, the League of Nations. "Chauvinistic nationalism is rampant," wrote one civil rights lawyer. "The hatred of everything that is foreign has become an obsession." By 1922, the Klan had as many as two million members. In 1923, the Supreme Court ruled that Bhagat Singh Thind, a Sikh American born in Punjab, India, who had served in the U.S. Army during the war, could not become a U.S. citizen because he was not white "in accordance with the understanding of the common man." The next year, the United States would all but shut its doors.

· XI ·

NATIONS AND ORIGINS

AMERICA OF THE MELTING POT COMES TO END, announced an eight-column headline in the *New York Times*. NORDIC VICTORY IS SEEN IN

DRASTIC REDUCTIONS, declared the *Los Angeles Times*. In 1924, Congress passed a two-part Immigration Act, banning immigration from anywhere in Asia, vastly restricting immigration from Europe, and sorting out European immigrants by their "national origins." Less eugenically desirable southern and eastern Europeans—Italians, Hungarians, and Jews—were all but barred entry.

The same year, in the Indian Citizenship Act, Congress granted citizenship to all native peoples in the United States, by fiat. The Indian Rights Association—an advocacy organization made up of white people—had lobbied for the act. Not all native peoples wanted it. The Onondaga protested the act as forced nationalization. Pueblo peoples had earlier asked to be excluded from laws that granted citizenship to men who had served in the First World War. Porfirio Mirabel of Taos told a House committee: "All that I ask the Government of the United States is that we want to be left alone and not to be made citizens."

Under the terms of both 1924 acts—the Immigration Act and the Indian Citizenship Act—becoming an American was not so much a matter of choice and consent but a matter of racial decree. Both acts were influenced by eugenicist tracts, especially Madison

Grant's *The Passing of the Great Race: Or, the Racial Basis of European History* (1916) and Lothrop Stoddard's *The Rising Tide of Color Against White World-Supremacy* (1920), and relied as well on a report prepared for Congress in 1911 that included a "Dictionary of Races or Peoples," which divided the world's peoples into "the white, black, yellow, brown, and red races," classing all but the first together as the "colored" or "dark" races. Many native people, asked to effectively become white by renouncing native nationhood and becoming U.S. citizens, refused.

The regime, nevertheless, proceeded. After 1924, immigrants to the United States were admitted on a system that established quotas based on national origin. Determining, on no basis whatsoever, that 75 percent of the population of the United States was descended from the eugenically preferable "Nordic," or northern European, stock, 75 percent of new immigrants had to be "Nordic," too. (This arrangement, which was less of a calculation that an act of imagination, specifically excluded from its computation all "descendants of slave immigrants," lest the proposed quota system "open the country to an African invasion.") The next year, in *Mein Kampf*, Adolf Hitler, who had read the first German edition of *The Pass-*

ing of the Great Race, applauded Americans' efforts at restricting immigration by "simply excluding certain races from naturalization."

Mexican immigrants stood as an exception to the 1924 act's quota regime. Especially after Mexico adopted a new constitution in 1917, its American consulate undertook to discourage the 1.5 million Mexicans who had emigrated into the United States between 1890 and 1929 from becoming Americans. Consular offices in California attempted to cultivate Mexican patriotism in hopes that migrant workers would return to Mexico. Meanwhile, American businesses that employed Mexicans tried just as hard to keep those Mexicans in the United States—if, preferably, not as citizens. They lobbied Congress to exclude Mexicans from the new immigration restriction regime by making their own racial arguments. W. H. Knox, of the Arizona Cotton Growers' Association, later said, "Have you ever heard, in the history of the United States, or in the history of the human race, of the white race being overrun by a class of people of the mentality of the Mexicans? I never have. We took this country from Mexico. Mexico did not take it from us." The businessmen won this argument—Mexicans were exempt from the National

Origins Act—but the 1930 Census nevertheless iden-
tified people of Mexican descent as "Mexican," and
Congress in 1924 established the U.S. Border Patrol
to guard the U.S.-Mexico border and check migrants
for papers authorizing their entry for purposes of
employment, making deportation of anyone deemed
an "illegal alien" U.S. policy, for the first time in
American history.

Somehow, long after the end of the Civil War, the
Union seemed to be losing to the Confederacy. In
1925, in a little-known answer to his far more famous
"The Significance of the Frontier in American History," Frederick Jackson Turner wrote an essay called
"The Significance of Sections in American History."
Given the persistence of sectionalism, American
nationalism had been southernized, Turner argued.
"The significance of the section in American history
is that it is the faint image of a European nation and
that we need to reexamine our history in light of this
fact," he wrote, describing Congress as not unlike the
League of Nations, a League of Sections.

Wilson's own internationalism, and likewise
FDR's, represented an extension of the natural logic
of liberal nationalism. So, arguably, did native peoples'
consideration of what came to be called the Indian

New Deal. Pressured by native rights activists, FDR's administration in the 1930s ended the Dawes allotment regime, set aside earlier federal policies, and moved—if haltingly, and by half measures—toward supporting native nationhood. "Let us try a new deal," the Okanogan writer Christine Quintasket, also known as Mourning Dove, urged native peoples who gathered in Oregon in 1934. "It cannot be any worse than what it has been."

During the Depression and into the Second World War, FDR rallied the nation behind his own patriotism, a celebration of American civic ideals in the form of four freedoms—freedom of speech, freedom of worship, freedom from want, and freedom from fear—a patriotism wholly consistent with his belief that the United States must engage in the affairs of the world. "Just as our national policy in internal affairs has been based upon a decent respect for the rights and the dignity of all our fellow men within our gates, so our national policy in foreign affairs has been based on a decent respect for the rights and the dignity of all nations, large and small," he told Congress.

Against Roosevelt's liberal nationalism stood an enduring illiberal nationalism, manifest as isolationism. In the 1930s, Hearst delivered his isolationist message over NBC Radio, warning that the nations of Europe were "all ready to go to war, and all eager to get us to go to war" but that "Americans should maintain the traditional policy of our great and independent nation—great largely because it is independent." Lothrop Stoddard traveled to Germany and met with Hitler. Grant's *The Passing of the Great Race* was reprinted seven times in the United States, including in 1930, 1932, and 1936; and in 1933 he published a new book, an American history called *The Conquest of a Continent*. "National problems today are, at bottom, race problems," read the book's ad copy. "Herr Hitler has stated that problem for Germany—and is working out his own solution. We in America have our own problem."

Grant's new book did not meet with the same success as his early work, but an American fringe nevertheless fervently supported Nazism. On the radio, Father Charles Coughlin preached anti-Semitism and admiration for Hitler and the Third Reich. To the extent that Hitler reciprocated, it was to express his admiration not for the United States but for the Confederacy, whose defeat in the Civil War he much regretted: "the beginnings of a great new social order based on the principle of slavery and inequality were destroyed by that war," he said. Nazi propagandists, sowing discord with radio broadcasts that the American press dubbed "fake news," tried to make common cause with white Southerners by urging the repeal of the Fourteenth and Fifteenth Amendments. Coughlin played into their hands. His audience heeded his call to form a new political party, the white nationalist Christian Front, in 1939, a year that twenty thousand Americans, some dressed in Nazi uniforms, gathered in Madison Square Garden, bedecked with swastikas and American flags, where they denounced the New Deal as the "Jew Deal" at a "Mass Demonstration for True Americanism."

America Firster Charles Lindbergh, who, not irrelevantly, had flown across the Atlantic, alone, based his nationalism in geography. "One need only glance at a map to see where our true frontiers lie," he said in 1939. "What more could we ask than the Atlantic Ocean on the east and the Pacific on the west?" This FDR answered in 1940, declaring the dream that the United States is "a lone island" to be, in fact, a nightmare, "the nightmare of a people lodged in prison, handcuffed, hungry, and fed through the bars from day to day by the contemptuous, unpitying masters of other continents."

In both Europe and the United States, a number of

intellectuals propped up the worst forms of national prejudice and national mythmaking and calls for acts of aggression in the name of national interest. Those "who indulged in this fanaticism betrayed their duty, which is precisely to set up a corporation whose sole cult is that of justice and of truth," the French philosopher Julien Benda argued in 1927, in *The Treason of the Intellectuals*. Madison Grant, who held no doctoral degree but went by the title "Dr. Grant" anyway, served on the board of the Museum of Natural History in New York. Lothrop Stoddard had earned a PhD—in history—at Harvard in 1914. A member of both the American Historical Association and the American Political Science Association, Stoddard delivered his white supremacy in the form of U.S. history books, including *Re-Forging America: The Story of Our Nationhood*, published in 1927.

The uglier and more illiberal nationalism got, the more liberal intellectuals became convinced of the impossibility of liberal nationalism. And yet in the 1930s, even as liberals in the United States despaired over the future of liberal democracy, they also exerted themselves to defend liberalism by confronting nationalism. Despite the treason of some intellectuals, growing numbers of American thinkers renounced eugenics and celebrated pluralism, and stood behind the United States as a nation of nations. In the best-selling *The Epic of America*, published in 1931, the historian James Truslow Adams introduced the idea of the "American dream," a phrase he coined. "That dream was not the product of a solitary thinker," Adams wrote. "It evolved from the hearts and burdened souls of many millions, who have come to us from all nations." Langston Hughes took that story and made it poetry. "Let America be the dream the dreamers dreamed," he wrote in 1935.

The land that never has been yet—
And yet must be—the land where every man is free.

And the WPA's Federal Theatre Project took *The Epic of America* and made it into a fourteen-part radio play broadcast across the United States and Canada. The next year, CBS Radio began broadcasting a twenty-six-week series called *Americans All—Immigrants All*, written by the journalist and critic Gilbert Seldes as part of a project initiated by FDR to celebrate "the many races and nationalities which make up our population." Most weeks it examined the history of a different ethnic group, declaring the United States "a pageant of all the nations." It was one of the first histories to reach a general audience with a reckoning with the history of slavery and white supremacy. In an age of *Amos 'n' Andy, Americans All—Immigrants All* advanced an idea of racial equality not often found on the radio, or in American popular culture more broadly. W. E. B. DuBois served as a consultant on the episode about "The Negro"—"the story of one immigrant who did not come of his own free will." He asked for more and better treatment of Frederick Douglass, African American artists, and white abolitionists. The program defined American history as "the story of magnificent adventure, the record of an unparalleled event in the history of mankind, in which millions of men and women from every country on the face of the earth, by their own choice and selection, became Americans and by so doing made the United States of America."

Stories like these had consequences. They made a new case for the nation. As the historian Oscar Handlin would later observe, "Somewhere, in the mid-1930s, there was a turn. Americans ceased to believe in race, the hate movements began to disintegrate, and discrimination increasingly took on the aspect of an anachronistic survival from the past rather than a pattern valid for the future." Handlin spoke too soon, but these efforts would continue during the Second World War. On December 15, 1941, Norman Corwin's *We Hold These Truths*, celebrating the 150th anniversary of the Bill of Rights, was broadcast live on all four major networks. "This is a program about the making of a promise and the keeping of a promise," narrator Lionel Barrymore announced. Its main character was played by Jimmy Stewart, five years before *It's a Wonderful Life*. An account of the history of the Bill of Rights, *We Hold These Truths* is a celebration of liberalism, and a challenge. "A promise is a promise. Has Americans' been kept? Has it come through peace and war, and peace and war, untarnished and unbroken?" Stewart asked. "Are the rights the right rights? . . . Who knows the answer better than the people?"

During the Second World War, Americans defended democracy abroad with fortitude and heroism. The war also challenged Americans' commitment to the nation's civic ideals. The day after Pearl Harbor, a University of California graduate of Japanese descent posted on the front of his grocery store at the corner of Eighth and Franklin Streets in Oakland a sign that read I AM AN AMERICAN. The next year, FDR signed an executive order that led to the imprisonment of more than 100,000 Japanese immigrants and Japanese Americans. Among those who protested was Gordon Hirabayashi, a senior at the University of Washington, who took his case to the Supreme Court. "I consider it my duty to maintain the democratic standards for which this nation lives," he said. "Distinctions between citizens solely because of their ancestry are by their very nature odious to a free people whose institutions are founded upon the doctrine of equality," the chief justice ruled in the majority opinion, but the court nevertheless upheld the restrictions, citing a national emergency. Still, Hirabayashi's protest would be passed down to a new generation of Asian American political activists. And fighting in the war opened other doors. "All of a sudden we became part of the American Dream," said Harold Liu, a Chinese American from New York. When places of business in Alaska posted signs reading "No Natives Allowed," Tlingit leaders Elizabeth and Roy Peratrovich wrote to the territorial governor, "Our Native boys are being called upon to defend our beloved country, just as the White boys." Their protest led, in the end, to Alaska's landmark 1945 Anti-Discrimination Act.

The nation would emerge from the war both stronger and in need of a new history. "Historians are to nationalism what poppy-growers . . . are to heroin-addicts," as the English historian Eric Hobsbawm once darkly observed. "We supply the essential raw material for the market." He was right. But you can also pick poppies for flowers, and make them into memorials for fallen soldiers.

· XII ·

COLD WAR LIBERALISM

The United Nations was established in 1945, a new league of nations. Three years later, its general assembly adopted a Universal Declaration of Human Rights. "All human beings are born free and equal in dignity and rights," it insisted, echoing the American Declaration of Independence. "They are endowed with reason and conscience and should act towards one another in a spirit of brotherhood." Historians started writing histories that could foresee this beginning as an ending. They needed to find an origin story for internationalism, and for human rights, and the triumph of liberalism. They also began writing histories that could explain the atrocities of the Second World War. They began to trace the origins of white nationalism.

John Higham began a history of American nativism in 1948, in an effort to understand "nationalism, that essential cement of modern societies that has so frightfully disrupted the modern world." That same year, Oscar Handlin attempted to reckon with the atrocity of the Holocaust—even before its scale was known—in *Race and Nationality in American Life*. "The frightful implications of the racism there expressed are an unforgettable part of Western history," Handlin wrote. For Handlin, the Holocaust itself required a new and even adversarial confrontation with American history: "Our own history shows that some of the sentiments that engage men's loyalties may find creative, rather than destructive, outlets in a nationalism free of restrictive and exclusive elements."

Yet Higham's and Handlin's approaches were unusual. Instead, especially after the Cold War began, American historians, keen to shore up Americanism in a Manichaean battle with communism, offered stories of ideological consensus rather than conflict, an account of a nearly unchallenged liberalism. They argued that Americans had never really been seduced by socialism as a way of insisting that Americans would never succumb to the influence of communism. They attacked Progressives like Charles Beard, rejecting his account of economic conflict and economic inequality. Arthur Schlesinger Jr., writing in 1949, insisted that liberals occupied "the vital center" of American politics. "In the United States at this time, liberalism is not only the dominant but even the sole intellectual tradition," Lionel Trilling argued, in *The Liberal Imagination* (1950). "For it is the plain fact that nowadays there are no conservative or reactionary ideas in general circulation." In 1955, in *The Liberal Tradition in America*, Louis Hartz attempted to chronicle an unvarying liberal tradition that appeared to stretch forward in time into an unvarying liberal future. That same year, in *The Age of Reform*, Richard Hofstadter offered a more complex assessment of the interplay between liberal and illiberal traditions, from populism to Progressivism. And, as Hofstadter famously wrote, in a review of Hartz's book, "It has been our fate as a nation not to have ideologies but to be one."

But this had not, in truth, been America's fate as a nation, nor would it be its future. In 1949, the year the United States entered the North Atlantic Treaty Organization, Hopi leaders wrote to President Truman, declaring the Hopi a sovereign nation and asking to be left out of the treaty. "We have heard about the Atlantic security treaty which we understood will bind the United States, Canada and six other European nations to an alliance in which an attack against one would be considered an attack against all," they wrote. "We will not bind ourselves to any foreign nation at this time. Neither will we go with you on a wild and reckless adventure which we know will lead us only to a total ruin."

This form of nationalism was largely ignored by American historians. So were other forms. Even as nationalism was on the rise in many parts of Africa, Asia, and Latin America, in nations that declared their independence after decades of colonial rule, scholars in Europe and the United States generally turned a blind eye. "The neglect of nationalism within the academy after 1945 is easily explained," as one scholar later observed. "Nationalism was blamed for the onset of war in 1939." *Nationalism and After* was the title of the English historian E. H. Carr's study of the subject in 1945, one of many early announcements of the end of nationalism. This neglect left American intellectuals particularly ill-equipped to confront the turmoil over *Brown v. Board of Education* after 1954, when white southerners began forming White Citizens' Councils to oppose desegregation, in the name of a white nation.

Cold War liberalism, for all its celebration of American civic ideals, turned only belatedly and inadequately to the question of civil rights. Schlesinger served as a speechwriter for two-time Democratic presidential candidate Adlai Stevenson. Accepting the nomination for the presidency in 1956, Stevenson called for a "New America." "I mean a New America, my friends, where freedom is made real for all without regard to race or belief or economic condition," he said. "I mean a New America which everlastingly attacks the ancient idea that men can solve their differences by killing each other." But Stevenson, despite being pressed by African Americans about his stance on civil rights, urged, at most, a gradualist approach. He lost to the Republican Dwight D. Eisenhower, twice. In 1958, the year Supreme Court Chief Justice Earl Warren defined citizenship as "man's basic right, for it is nothing less than the right to have rights," John F. Kennedy, a senator from Massachusetts, would offer his own story of the American dream, in a book called *A Nation of Immigrants.* Commissioned by the Anti-Defamation League, much of the book was prepared by one of Oscar Handlin's former doctoral students. But Kennedy's ghostwriters ignored Handlin's critique of American immigration policy, and in the end, *A Nation of Immigrants* failed to confront the conflation of race and nation.

Midcentury liberals like Hofstadter and Schlesinger made an argument—*This is what America means . . .*—and they defended it. They didn't offer catechisms. They offered interpretations that were worth arguing over. By no means were the histories written by these men unerring; the blind spots of a historical profession composed almost entirely of white men made for a view more obstructed than clear. But if these historians and critics had their blind spots, and they had many, they were nevertheless doing the work of attempting to offer an expansive, liberal account of the history of the American nation and the American people, in ways that proved meaningful and important and lasting, and especially powerful in the struggle against McCarthyism.

Still, they never really reckoned with the depth of the American divide. And by the 1950s, that divide was tearing the nation apart. "If I have to choose between the United States government and Mississippi, then I'll choose Mississippi," William Faulkner said in an interview in 1956. "What I'm trying to do now is not to have to make that decision. As long as there's a middle road, all right. I'll be on it. But if it came to fighting I'd fight for Mississippi against the United States even if it meant going out into the street and shooting Negroes." By then, another reign of terror had begun.

· XIII ·

CAN THIS
BE AMERICA?

On Friday, May 9, 1958, Rabbi Jacob M. Rothschild, of the Hebrew Benevolent Congregation in Atlanta, delivered a sermon called "Can This Be America?" White nationalists—terrorists—had burned crosses and lynched men across the South, but what Rothschild was talking about was mainly the bombs: bundled sticks of dynamite tied to coiled fuses. In 1956, a bomb misfired at Martin Luther King Jr.'s home in Montgomery. From March 1957 to March 1958 alone, white nationalists had set bombs, or tried to set bombs, at forty-seven places—at black churches, at white schools that had begun to admit black children, at an auditorium where Louis Armstrong was playing. Most were directed at African Americans, attempts to shatter the very institutions that hold societies, and nations, together: schools, churches, newspapers. One out of every ten attacks was directed at Jews, at synagogues and community centers in Charlotte, in Nashville, in Jacksonville, in Birmingham. In March 1958, some twenty sticks of dynamite, wrapped in paper yarmulkes, had exploded in an Orthodox temple in Miami. The blast sounded like a plane crash. "Our first duty is not to allow ourselves to be intimidated," Rothschild told his congregation that May. Five months later, fifty or so sticks of dynamite exploded at Rothschild's temple, Atlanta's oldest synagogue, on Peachtree Street, blowing a twenty-foot hole in a brick wall, toppling columns and shattering stained glass windows. "We bombed a temple in Atlanta," a man claiming to be from "the Confederate Underground" said when he telephoned the press that night: "Negroes and Jews are hereby declared aliens."

Jacob Rothschild had grown up in Pittsburgh, in Squirrel Hill. He was raised in Temple Rodef Shalom, which is just blocks away from the Tree of Life syna-

gogue, where, in 2018, forty-six-year-old truck driver
Robert Bowers was arrested and charged with shooting and killing eleven people during services. Bowers
had repeatedly posted on social media about a Jewish aid organization he thought was helping refugees
cross the U.S.-Mexico border. This atrocity followed
a series of mail bombs sent to critics of President
Trump, allegedly by Cesar Sayoc Jr., a fifty-six-year-
old Florida man who lived in a white van plastered
with Trump stickers. In the days after the mail bombs
and the mass shooting, Trump announced his intention to end birthright citizenship, to declare, by executive order, that U.S.-born children of undocumented
immigrants are aliens.

Rothschild, the liberal from Pittsburgh, had moved
to Atlanta to take the pulpit in 1946, the year that
a white supremacist organization was founded in the
city. The Columbians, undercutting the ten-dollar
membership fee levied by the Klan, asked potential
members three questions: "Do you hate Negroes? Do
you hate Jews? Do you have three dollars?" On Yom
Kippur in 1948, Rothschild had chided his congregation for its silence. "There is only one real issue," he
said. "Civil rights."

The reign of terror Rothschild decried in his ser-

mon in 1958 had begun in 1954, after the Supreme
Court's decision in *Brown v. Board of Education*, which
made racial segregation in public schools unconstitutional. Mayor William B. Hartsfield, standing at
the site of the Atlanta temple blast, declared, "Every
political rabble-rouser is the godfather of these cross
burners and dynamiters who sneak about in the dark
and give a bad name to the South." President Eisenhower declared that the "Confederate Underground"
was an insult to "the good name of the Confederacy."
In the *Atlanta Constitution*, the syndicated columnist
Ralph McGill wrote: "To be sure, none said go bomb
a Jewish temple or a school. But let it be understood
that when leadership in high places in any degree fails
to support constituted authority, it opens the gates
to all those who wish to take law into their hands."
The FBI investigated and five men were arrested. The
American Nationalist, a California newspaper, ran a
story that announced, "SYNAGOGUE BOMBING A
FRAUD: Jewish Groups Use Bomb Incident to Confuse Gentiles." Only one man, George Bright, was
ever tried; he was acquitted. McGill won a Pulitzer
Prize. "If you call that a prize," Bright scoffed. "Pulitzer was just a Jew."

The twenty-first-century American reign of terror,

its resurgent, illiberal nationalism, the nationalism of the *American Nationalist*, began not with Trump's election in 2016 but with Obama's in 2008, the *Brown v. Board* of the presidency. "Impeach Obama," read the yard signs. "He's Unconstitutional." In March of 2011, Trump first began publicly demanding that Obama prove his citizenship. "I feel I have accomplished something really, really important," Trump told the press, when the White House offered up the president's birth certificate a month later. In 2018, Massachusetts Senator Elizabeth Warren fell into the same trap. After Trump hounded her for years about her claim of Cherokee ancestry, Warren had her DNA analyzed. Obama's birth certificate didn't quiet Trump, and neither did Warren's DNA test. What he was after was asserting his right to question the birthright citizenship and racial ancestry of his political opponents, and by supplying that birth certificate, and that DNA test, they seemed to acknowledge his right to ask for them. For the five years of his long campaign for the nation's attention, leading up to the 2016 election, and for the first years of his administration, attempts to fight Trump with Trump's methods only strengthened him.

In 1958, Rothschild preached to his congregation

the Friday after the bombing. He announced the title of the sermon he intended to give on a bulletin board, down the hill from the temple, by the road. He had taken his title from the Book of Micah: "And None Shall Make Them Afraid." Eight hundred people crowded into the blasted synagogue. "Never did a band of violent men so misjudge the temper of the objects of their act of intimidation," Rothschild said. "For this is what really happened: Out of the gaping hole that laid bare the havoc wrought within, out of the majestic columns that now lay crumbled and broken, out of the tiny bits of brilliantly colored glass that had once graced with beauty the sanctuary itself— indeed, out of the twisted and evil hearts of bestial men has come a new courage and a new hope."

Courage and hope were not the language of Trump's most vociferous political opponents. Blame and grievance were their language, the language of the times, the grammar of Twitter, the idiom of Trump, the taste of bile in every mouth. Trump's loudest critics answered Trump's viciousness with their own viciousness, his abandonment of norms with their own abandonment, his unwillingness to speak to the whole of the country with their own parochialism, speaking to their own followers rather than to the nation, and blanching at expressions of love of country.

But the violence and bloody-mindedness of deranged and broken men can only be countered by principle, and fortitude, and by unerring means. That fortitude includes making appeals to national ends, and making the case for the nation.

Rothschild once introduced Martin Luther King Jr. at a banquet in Chicago. King, he said, was received with "wild thunder." In the 1960s, King called on the oratory of Lincoln at Gettysburg. He invoked the tradition forged by Frederick Douglass, calling for a composite nation. He called on the language of the "American dream" from James Truslow Adams's *Epic of America*. In 1962, King spoke at the Emanuel African Methodist Episcopal Church in Charleston, South Carolina, leading a rally for voting rights to make "the American dream a reality." In 2015, a twenty-one-year-old white man named Dylann Roof would enter that same church and shoot and kill nine people. Roof, an avowed white supremacist who photographed himself with Confederate regalia, said he wanted to start another civil war.

The shootings and bombings in Atlanta in 1958, Charleston in 2015, and Pittsburgh in 2018 testified to the endurance of racial hatred. But the reaction to them also testified to the strength of other forms of belonging. In 1963, at the March on Washington marking the hundredth anniversary of the Emancipation Proclamation, King had said, "I have a dream that one day this nation will rise up and live out the true meaning of its creed: 'We hold these truths to be self-evident, that all men are created equal.'" Never did King speak with more thunder than during what would be his last Christmas Eve sermon, in 1967, at the Ebenezer Baptist Church in Atlanta, down the road from Rothschild's temple. "If we don't have good will toward men in this world, we will destroy ourselves," King said that day. "There have always been those who argued that the end justifies the means, that the means really aren't important," he said. "But we will never have peace in the world until men everywhere recognize that ends are not cut off from means, because the means represent the ideal in the making, and the end in process, and ultimately you can't reach good ends through evil means, because the means represent the seed and the end represents the tree." Another tree had been cut down. A new seed would have to be sown.

· XIV ·

THE END
OF LIBERALISM?

The last best single-volume history of the United States published in the twentieth century was written by Carl Degler, in 1959. *Out of Our Past: The Forces That Shaped Modern America*, a stunning, sweeping account that, much influenced by DuBois, places race, slavery, segregation, and civil rights at the center of its story, alongside liberty, rights, revolution, freedom, and equality, was Degler's first book. (It had plenty of limitations. It contained, Degler admitted, "no mention of the American Indians.") It was also the last of its kind.

If love of the nation had driven American historians to the study of the past in the nineteenth century, hatred for nationalism drove American historians away from it in the second half of the twentieth century. That nationalism is a contrivance, an artifice, a fiction, had long been clear. After the Second World War, even as Roosevelt was helping to establish what came to be called the liberal world order, internationalists began predicting the end of the nation-state, Harvard political scientist Rupert Emerson declaring "that the nation and the nation-state are anachronisms in the atomic age." By the 1960s, an era marked by a rising tide of anti-Americanism, the nation-state looked rather worse than an anachronism.

"We don't even have a country," a young black man in San Francisco said to James Baldwin in 1963. "I question America," civil rights leader Fannie Lou Hamer said at the Democratic National Convention, challenging the credentials committee to seat the Mississippi Freedom Democratic Party delegation. Liberalism could not contain the critique of the nation that civil rights demanded. "Is this America," Hamer asked, "where we have to sleep with our telephones off the hooks because our lives be threatened daily, because we want to live as decent human beings, in America?" After decades of white liberals' failures to confront race, black nationalism surged. "I'm not a Democrat. I'm not a Republican, and I don't even consider myself an American," Malcolm X said in 1964, a month after he'd left the Nation of Islam. "If you and I were Americans, there'd be no problem. Those

Honkies that just got off the boat, they're already Americans; Polacks are already Americans; the Italian refugees are already Americans. Everything that came out of Europe, every blue-eyed thing, is already an American. And as long as you and I have been over here, we aren't Americans yet."

Indian rights activists, distinguishing their objectives from those of the civil rights movement, continued to press for more than one way of understanding what a nation is, and for forms of belonging other than assimilation. In 1965, Standing Rock Sioux Vine Deloria Jr., the new head of the National Congress of American Indians, spoke to a Senate committee considering the question of constitutional rights and native peoples. "This organization I run is kind of a miniature United Nations with everybody taking his shoe off and hammering on the desk," he said, pressing the comparison. "All we basically ask is justice, the consent of the governed, time to develop what we think should be developed in our own way."

The same year, in the shadow of the Statue of Liberty on Liberty Island, Lyndon Johnson signed the 1965 Immigration and Nationality Act. He had announced that "a nation that was built by immigrants of all lands can ask those who now seek admission: 'What can you do for our country?' But we should not be asking: 'In what country were you born?'"

The 1965 Immigration Act came quick on the heels of the 1964 Civil Rights Act and the 1965 Voting Rights Act, which were meant to realize the promise of the Fourteenth and Fifteenth Amendments. The new immigration regime abolished the national origins-based quota system that had been instituted in the Immigration Act of 1924 and replaced it with an evenly distributed quota system of 20,000 immigrants per country, per year, with a maximum of 170,000 annual immigrants from the Eastern Hemisphere and, later, 120,000 from the Western Hemisphere; it extended the principle of political equality from citizens to immigrants. "It corrects a cruel and enduring wrong in the conduct of the American Nation," said Johnson.

The Immigration Act marked a brief midcentury reunification of liberalism and nationalism. It represented the culmination of decades of pressure to overturn a regime that, among other things, had led the United States to close its doors to Jews fleeing the Holocaust in the 1930s and the millions of Europeans displaced during and after the Second World War. Organized efforts to overturn the 1924 act had begun in 1952, when Truman established a Commission on Immigration and Naturalization. New York senator Herbert Lehman (for whom Oscar Handlin served as an adviser) testified before the commission that the national origins quota system "is based on the same discredited racial theories from which Adolf Hitler developed the infamous Nuremberg laws. . . . It is the complete denial of Americanism." Earlier, and especially in a 1947 essay called "Democracy Needs the Open Door," Handlin had argued for unrestricted immigration. But as the historian Mae Ngai has pointed out, most liberals who fought for the 1965 Immigration Act no longer questioned the idea of immigration restriction itself; they merely changed the way restriction worked. They treated the idea of immigration restriction as if it were a timeless American tradition, when in fact, like the national origins regime itself, it was only forty years old.

A liberal dream of a better America was derailed by Johnson's commitment to waging a war in Vietnam, which divided the country and set in motion the political polarization that diminished liberalism by spurring the rise of both a New Left and a New Right.

"Power tends to confuse itself with virtue and a great nation is peculiarly susceptible to the idea that power is a sign of God's favor, conferring upon it a special responsibility for other nations," wrote Senator J. William Fulbright in 1966. The horrors of Vietnam and the brutality of attacks on civil rights activists and African American institutions, which included the bombing of churches and the murder of little girls, cast the nature of the American nation into doubt. So did American history. Wrote Vine Deloria Jr. in 1971, "White citizens, worrying over the increasing brutality of the American forces in Southeast Asia should ponder the story of the Indian wars and re-examine their unshakeable faith that America is always engaged in handing out candy bars to the children of its victims." In that same spirit, American historians within the academy looked to those Indian wars, and to the history of slavery and segregation, and called for an end to the study of the nation, in part, out of a fear of complicity—complicity with the atrocities of U.S. foreign policy and complicity with regimes of political oppression at home. If nationalism was a pathology, the thinking went, the writing of national histories was one of its symptoms.

The death of nationalism had been the dream of

internationalists at least since the introduction of the League of Nations in 1918. A half century after that founding, the dream began, to some, to seem like a real possibility. The Foreign Policy Association had been founded in 1918 to advance the international-ism represented by the League of Nations. In 1968, to mark its fiftieth anniversary, the association published a collection of essays called *Toward the Year 2018,* a book of predictions about what the world would look like in fifty years' time. In that collection, MIT polit-ical scientist Ithiel de Sola Pool prophesied that as "better communication, easier translation, and greater understanding of the nature of human motivations make it common for people to react to each other as human to human, across ethnic and national lines," one development appeared almost inevitable: "the waning of nationalism."

But something else was going on, too. Studying the nation began to fall out of favor in the historical pro-fession in the 1960s just when women and people of color entered the PhD programs in sizable numbers for the first time. They brought to the study of his-tory an altogether different vantage, that of people deprived of political equality for centuries, and whose relationship to the nation-state and especially to nationalism had been, from the start, vexed. As James Baldwin observed in 1962, "The American Negro has the great advantage of having never believed that collection of myths to which white Americans cling: that their ancestors were all freedom-loving heroes, that they were born in the greatest country the world has ever seen, or that Americans are invincible in battle and wise in peace." Baldwin called for an honest reckoning. So did Rodolfo Gonzales, a leader of the Chicano movement, who in 1969 led a walkout at a Denver high school to protest unequal treatment and the exclusion of Mexican American history from the teaching of the nation's past. Gonzales argued for "the inclusion in all schools of this city the history of our people, our culture, language, and our contributions to this country." So did Vine Deloria Jr., especially in his best-selling manifesto *Custer Died for Your Sins*, published in 1969, the year the Indians of All Tribes began a nearly nineteen-month-long protest at Alcatraz. So did women's historians and gay rights activists. And so did the long-silenced voices shouting out from the archives of American history.

Beginning in the 1970s, a new generation of academic historians either investigated the experiences of the very many people and peoples left out of earlier

American histories, a scholarship that both emerged out of and carried on decades-long struggles for political equality, or else they took the sweeping vantage promised by global history, which carried its own urgency in an era of global climate change. Those approaches produced essential scholarship, searching and vital.

American historical scholarship exploded, and got immeasurably richer and more sophisticated. Degler, a white man who was one of two male founders of the National Organization for Women, wrote about women and about race—he won a Pulitzer in 1972 for a book called *Neither Black nor White*—but most historians who wrote about race were not white, and most historians who wrote about women were not men. In the 1990s, American historical scholarship also got more fractured, more theoretical, more abstract, and more obscure. While American historians continued to study the United States, John Higham argued in 1994, their work was "not about the United States but merely in the United States." Four years later, Janice Radway, president of the American Studies Association, would question the "notion of a bounded national territory and a concomitant national identity deriving isomorphically from it" and wonder whether "the perpetuation of the particular name, 'American,' in the title of the field and in the name of the association continue surreptitiously to support the notion that such a whole exists."

But if American Studies no longer seemed to exist, the United States still did. And it was undergoing dramatic changes. The 1965 Immigration Act reopened America's borders. Between 1931 and 1965, five and a half million immigrants entered the United States; more than nine million entered in the 1990s alone. Less than 5 percent of the U.S. population had been foreign-born in 1970; 11 percent would be in 2000. That rate wasn't as high as it had been before the First World War, when the percentage of the U.S. population that was foreign-born reached 14 percent. But it was still higher than it had been in most Americans' lifetimes. Newer immigrants, unlike earlier waves of immigrants, came mostly from Asia and Latin America. By 1971, immigrants from Asia would outnumber those from Europe. Just over one million in 1965, the Asian American population of the United States had risen by 2000 to more than ten million. And, as had been the case with the 1924 National Origins Act, the 1965 Immigration Act had unusual consequences for immigrants from Mexico. In 1964, the United States closed the Bracero Program, under which some 4.5

million Mexican men had come to the United States from Mexico as guest workers. Mexican immigrants, who had been exempt from the quota system of the 1924 act, now fell under a numerical limit, a cap of 20,000 immigrants per year, which amounted to a 40 percent reduction in legal immigration from Mexico. Millions of Mexicans continued to cross the border for temporary work but now began to do so without papers and found themselves unable to cross back and forth easily. Between 1965 and 1986, an estimated twenty-eight million Mexicans arrived in the United States without papers, belonging, as many said, *"ni de aquí ni de allá"*—from neither here nor there. A 1986 Immigration Reform and Control Act opened a path to citizenship for many undocumented immigrants but also made going back and forth across the border without papers even more difficult, leaving millions of undocumented immigrants who by now had formed families all but trapped in the United States, which they came to call the *jaula de oro*, the Cage of Gold.

Between 1965 and 2000, conservatism became the dominant force in American politics. Conservatives attacked liberalism, they attacked the press, they attacked the academy. They took over the GOP and won the White House, Congress, and the Supreme Court.

Most Republicans weren't nationalists and in fact repudiated nationalism. But Trump was a nationalist with a vengeance. Liberals and the Left offered answers, but few of them involved the nation, as a nation.

In 1986, when Degler rose from his chair to deliver his presidential address before the American Historical Association, hardly anyone in the academy was writing national history anymore, or making the case for the nation. Degler didn't have much patience with this. Nor, I suspect, did he have much patience with Francis Fukuyama's 1989 "The End of History?" Later, after the onset of civil war in Bosnia, the political theorist Michael Walzer grimly announced, "The tribes have returned." They had never left. They'd only become harder for historians to see, because they weren't really looking anymore.

· XV ·

THE RETURN OF NATIONALISM

To say that events did not bear out foretellings of the death of nationalism is to mute the screams of millions. Events hacked up such predictions with a machete; they rolled over them with tanks; they burned them with torches. "We soon found out how wrong we were," Michael Ignatieff wrote, in a mournful book called *Blood and Belonging*, in 1993, while Bosnian Muslims were subjected to a war of "ethnic cleansing" that would lead to the displacement of more than two million people and whose atrocities included the rape of as many as fifty thousand women. "With blithe lightness of mind, we assumed that the world was moving irrevocably beyond nationalism, beyond tribalism, beyond the provincial confines of the identities inscribed in our passports, toward a global market culture which was to be our new home," Ignatieff wrote. "In retrospect, we were whistling in the dark. The repressed has returned, and its name is nationalism."

In 1994, the year of the North American Free Trade Agreement, a year when the roads of Rwanda ran red with rivers of blood in a war that took the lives of as many as a million Rwandans and left some two million as refugees, and another million and a half displaced, the historian Tony Judt would ask, "Who now believes in the idyllic prospect held out before our eyes in the late 1980s, the dream of a prosperous,

united (Western) Europe, shorn of frontiers, passports, and conflicts?" No one. Except, weirdly, by the
1990s, the dewy-eyed promoters of the internet. In
the spring of 2000, *Wired* magazine announced that
"partisanship, religion, geography, race, gender, and
other traditional political divisions are giving way to
a new standard—wiredness—as an organizing principle." They soon found out how wrong they were.

The United States, thought by some to have never
known nationalism, was now said to be beyond
nationalism. A politics of identity replaced a politics
of nationality. In the end, they weren't very different
from each other. Nor did identity politics dedicate
a new generation of intellectuals to the study of the
nation or a new generation of Americans to a broader
understanding of Americanism.

Many native peoples, all this while, were in fact
making the case for the nation. They were reimag-
ining the nation-state. They were building native
nations. They were abdicating a nationality of blood.
In an age of surging blood-and-soil American nationalism, native nations like Osage, repudiating centuries
of racial measurement regimes that had purported
to identify "full-bloods," "half-bloods," and "mixed
bloods," formally disavowed the measure of "blood

quantum" as a requirement for membership in the nation.

Who belongs in a nation? Who decides? In an age of worldwide refugee crises, many called for a new understanding of citizenship and a new ethics of immigration. As the philosopher Kwame Anthony Appiah observed in 1997, "the system of states means that all individuals in the world are obliged, whether they like it or not, to accept the political arrangements of their birthplace—however repugnant those arrangements are to their principles or ambitions—unless they can persuade somebody else to let them in." The time had come to rethink the nature of borders and, in particular, their histories. For Appiah, the question to ask was not what the American founders thought about these questions but whether the founders were right. "If they were right, then we can agree with them; if they are wrong, we must reject them. What matters, surely, is what is right."

In a newly conservative country, immigration now stood at the center of American politics. By the 1990s, the debate over immigration had grown as intense as the one that had raged in the 1910s and 1920s. The undocumented Mexican immigrant population of the United States rose from about one million in 1988 to more than six and a half million in 2008. The U.S.-Mexico border became more militarized, and more dangerous, with Operation Blockade in Texas in 1993 and Operation Gatekeeper in California in 1994. In 1997, the chair of a congressional Commission on Immigration Reform said that immigration "is about who and what we are as a Nation," a common refrain. Few had answers. But immigration became, increasingly, the issue on which American politics turned. Between 2005 and 2013, at least one person a day on average died trying to cross into the United States from Mexico.

The end of the Cold War didn't kill nationalism. Global trade didn't kill nationalism. Immigration reform didn't kill nationalism. The internet didn't kill nationalism. Instead, arguably, all of these developments only stoked nationalism. And so, in the United States, did the attacks on September 11, 2001. The next day, President George W. Bush announced the beginning of "a monumental struggle of good versus evil." In the aftermath, much of the Left expressed withering disdain for a renewed spirit of patriotism. "The globe, not the flag, is the symbol that's wanted now," wrote Katha Pollitt in the *Nation*.

But what about the future of the nation? In *Liberal*

Nationalism, Yael Tamir, a political philosopher and peace activist and Israel's former Minister of Immigrant Absorption, argued that "the liberal tradition, with its respect for personal autonomy, reflection, and choice, and the national tradition, with its emphasis on belonging, loyalty, and solidarity, although generally seen as mutually exclusive, can indeed accommodate one another." Plenty of political theorists and historians found this unpersuasive. The political scientist Judith Shklar, who had fled Riga in Latvia as a child before the German invasion, is among many learned commentators who, although she acknowledged the virtue of what she described as "restrained patriotism," deemed liberal nationalism to be an oxymoron. The philosopher Martha Nussbaum described patriotism as "morally dangerous." Tony Judt, an English-born NYU historian who had once been a Zionist, admired the idea of a liberal nationalism but believed that it was essentially nothing more than a thought experiment. A well-meaning person could imagine such a thing, he allowed, but no one could point to anyplace on the map where it actually existed. And, as a thought experiment, he found it silly. "If we have no prior grounds for imagining a world divided in the ways ours is, would we really invent such divisions, however liberal, as the best way of proceeding?"

Judt was probably right. If nation-states didn't already exist, they wouldn't really be a great thing to invent. But they do exist. It's no use pretending people don't live in nations, or that the age of the nation-state is over, or about to end. Nor is it any use pretending that nations are without error, or fortresses impenetrable, or destined for greatness. Nation-states are people with a common past, often a mythical one, who live under the rule of a government in the form of a state. Liberal nations are people who understand themselves as individual political equals, each with an equal right to participate in government. By pretending nations are more or less than these things, nothing is to be gained except self-deception and the inheritance of misery. And whether nations can remain liberal actually depends on the recovery of the many ways of understanding what it means to belong to a nation, and even to love a nation, the place, the people, and the idea itself.

In American history, liberals have failed, time and again, to defeat illiberalism except by making appeals to national aims and ends. As Michael Kazin argued passionately in 2002, "Having abandoned patriotism, the left lost the ability to pose convincing alternatives for the nation as a whole." Appeals to nationalism are dangerous. But not thinking about the nation, and not learning from how all of the people in the United States have thought about the nation, is more dangerous. Writing national history creates plenty of problems. But not writing national history creates more problems, and those problems are worse.

During the decades when many serious American historians stopped writing national history, scorned patriotism, and abandoned the defense of American civic ideals, Americans interested in a national story read other sorts of books. In 2005, Lynne Cheney, the wife of the former vice president, produced a book of dates comprising "our national story." *The 5,000 Year Leap: 28 Great Ideas That Changed the World*, written in 1981 by a John Bircher named W. Cleon Skousen, was reissued in 2009 with a foreword by Fox News's Glenn Beck; it sold more than two hundred fifty thousand copies in just the first half of that year, the beginning of Obama's presidency. Fox News's Bill O'Reilly began writing U.S. history books in 2011, starting with *Killing Lincoln*, telling the story of the nation as a carnage. From *Killing Lincoln* he moved on to writing "killing" books about people who hadn't actually ever been killed. "O'Reilly's vast carelessness pollutes history and debases the historian's craft," the conservative columnist George F. Will wrote in the *Washington Post* in 2013. But by then O'Reilly's history books had already sold 6.8 million copies. Donald Trump's onetime chief strategist Steve Bannon admired a dystopian 1997 book called *The Fourth Turning: An American Prophecy*, by William Strauss and Neil Howe. "This is a book that turns history into prophecy," its authors boasted. That prophecy? The fourth turning "could mark the end of man," or "the end of modernity," or it "could spare modernity but mark the end of our nation," or it "could find America, and the world, a much better place." Bannon turned the book into a documentary film, in 2010, in which he described a vast left-wing conspiracy to destroy capitalism. Quoting the book, the film ended with the warning that "history is seasonal, and winter is coming."

A different winter came. Trump demanded Obama's birth certificate. He launched his campaign in 2015 with a promise to build a wall on the U.S.-Mexico border, at a time when more Mexicans were returning to Mexico from the United States than were coming here; net migration was negative. (Since 2007, undocumented Mexican migration had fallen by more than 75 percent. And despite the rise in Central American migration, overall Border Patrol apprehensions were at their second lowest level in more than four decades.) Days after Trump took office, he authorized the completion of the Dakota Access Pipeline, waving aside any native claims to sovereignty. He also demanded that Elizabeth Warren—a U.S. senator he called "Pocahontas"—prove her native ancestry. In the first years of his presidency, he called for a regime of deportation of undocumented immigrants. He instituted a plan to separate immigrant children from their parents. He banned immigrants from Muslim-majority countries. His administration asked the U.S. Census Bureau to add to the 2020 Census the question "Is this person a citizen of the United States?" He shut down the government for more than a month when Congress failed to fund his plan to build a wall between the United States and Mexico. He announced his intention to end birthright citizenship. He called his political opponents globalists. He asked his supporters to call themselves nationalists. *"Use that word!"*

Winter came. Winter always comes. But, invariably, then comes spring.

· XVI ·

A NEW AMERICANISM

The United States is a nation founded on a revolutionary, generous, and deeply moral commitment to human equality and dignity. In the very struggles that constitute this nation's history, in the very struggles that lie ahead, the United States holds to these truths: all of us are equal, we are equal as citizens, and we are equal under the law. For all the agony of the nation's past, these truths remain. Anyone who affirms these truths and believes that we should govern our common life together belongs in this country. That is America's best idea.

Frederick Douglass once offered his understanding of this nation: "A Government founded upon justice, and recognizing the equal rights of all men; claiming no higher authority for its existence, or sanction for

its laws, than nature, reason, and the regularly ascer-
tained will of the people; steadily refusing to put its
sword and purse in the service of any religious creed
or family, is a standing offense to most of the Governments of the world, and to some narrow and bigoted
people among ourselves." These words are no less true
a century and a half on.

Americans are bound by our past, but even more
powerfully, we are bound to one another. A new
Americanism would have to honor the striving and
sacrifices of Americans whose families have been in
the United States for generations, and those who have
only just arrived. It would have to honor the sovereignty of native nations. It would have to uphold the
aspirations of everyone. In 2011, the Pulitzer Prize–
winning journalist Jose Antonio Vargas, an undocumented immigrant, began asking immigrants and the
children of immigrants to define "American": "I define
American as my family," said one little girl. A nation is
that collection of definitions. This America is a community of belonging and commitment, held together
by the strength of our ideas and by the force of our
disagreements. A nation founded on universal ideas
will never stop fighting over the meaning of its past
and the direction of the future. That doesn't mean the

past or future is meaningless, or directionless, or that anyone can afford to sit out the fight. The nation, as ever, *is* the fight.

In a world made up of nations, there is no more powerful way to fight the forces of prejudice, intolerance, and injustice than by a dedication to equality, citizenship, and equal rights, as guaranteed by a nation of laws. A new Americanism would mean a devotion to equality and liberty, tolerance and inquiry, justice and fairness, along with a commitment to national prosperity inseparable from an unwavering dedication to a sustainable environment the world over. It would require a clear-eyed reckoning with American history, its sorrows no less than its glories. A lie stands on one foot, as Benjamin Franklin liked to say, but a truth stands upon two. A new Americanism would rest on a history that tells the truth, as best it can, about what W. E. B. DuBois called the hideous mistakes, the frightful wrongs, and the great and beautiful things that nations do. It would foster a spirit of citizenship and environmental stewardship and a set of civic ideals, and a love of one another, marked by benevolence and hope and a dedication to community and honesty. Looking both backward and forward, it would know that right wrongs no man.

"The history of the United States at the present time does not seek to answer any significant questions," Carl Degler told an audience of historians some three decades ago. Degler, like all of us, had his own blind spots. But he did not sit out the struggle. And if people who care about the nation's past and future and the endurance of liberal democratic nations don't start asking and answering those sorts of questions, he warned, other people will. They'll declare America a carnage. They'll call immigrants "animals" and other countries "shitholes." They call themselves "nationalists." They'll say they can make America great again. Their history will be a fiction. They will say that they alone love this country. They will be wrong.

ACKNOWLEDGMENTS

Daniel Kurtz-Phelan at *Foreign Affairs* invited me to write the essay that became this book. Jane Kamensky read an early draft. Bob Weil at Norton asked me to turn that essay into a book. Tina Bennett gave me a much-needed kick in the pants. Heartfelt thanks to all. My deep thanks, too, to Henry Finder at *The New Yorker*, as ever. I am particularly grateful to four generous colleagues who read the manuscript and provided essential comments on very short notice: Philip Deloria, Michael Katz, Sanford Levinson, and Charles Maier. Don Rifkin and Janet Byrne shepherded the manuscript through production. Emily Gogolak expertly checked facts. Any outstanding errors are my own. Thanks as well to the readers of my last book, *These Truths*, who wrote to me asking the hard questions that convinced me to write this book.

SELECTED SOURCES

Anderson, Benedict. *Imagined Communities: Reflections on the Origins and Spread of Nationalism*. New York: Verso, 1991.

Appiah, Kwame Anthony. "Citizenship in Theory and Practice: A Response to Charles Kesler." In Pickus, *Immigration and Citizenship in the Twenty-First Century*, 41–47.

Armitage, David. "Interchange: Nationalism and Internationalism in the Era of the Civil War." *Journal of American History* 98 (2011): 455–89.

Beeman, Richard, Stephen Botein, and Edward C. Carter II, eds. *Beyond Confederation: Origins of the Constitution and American National Identity*. Chapel Hill: University of North Carolina Press, 1987.

Bender, Thomas. *Rethinking American History in a Global Age*. Berkeley: University of California Press, 2002.

Beiner, Ronald, ed. *Theorizing Nationalism*. Albany: State University of New York Press, 1999.

Carr, E. H. *Nationalism and After*. London: Macmillan, 1945.

Cobb, Daniel M. *Say We Are Nations: Documents of Politics and Protest in Indigenous America Since 1887*. Chapel Hill: University of North Carolina Press, 2015.

Colley, Linda. *Britons: Forging the Nation, 1707–1837*. New Haven, CT: Yale University Press, 1992.

Degler, Carl N. "In Pursuit of an American History." *American Historical Review* 92 (February 1987): 1–12.

Deloria, Vine, Jr., ed. *Of Utmost Good Faith*. San Francisco: Straight Arrow Books, 1971.

Doyle, Don, and Marco Antonio Pamplona, eds. *Nationalism in the New World*. Athens: University of Georgia Press, 2006.

Dossett, Kate. *Bridging Race Divides: Black Nationalism, Feminism, and Integration in the United States, 1896–1935*. Gainesville: University Press of Florida, 2008.

DuBois, W. E. B. *Black Reconstruction in America*. New York: Free Press, 1935.

Epps, Garrett. *Democracy Reborn: The Fourteenth Amendment and the Fight for Equal Rights in Post–Civil War America*. New York: Henry Holt, 2006.

Fukuyama, Francis. "The End of History?" *The National Interest*, Summer 1989.

———. *Identity: The Demand for Dignity and the Politics of Resentment*. New York: Farrar, Straus and Giroux, 2018.

Gates, Henry, Jr. *Stony the Road: Reconstruction, White Supremacy, and the Rise of Jim Crow*. New York: Penguin, 2019.

Gellner, Ernest. *Nations and Nationalism*. 2nd ed. London: Blackwell, 2006. First published in 1983.

Gerstle, Gary. *American Crucible: Race and Nation in the Twentieth Century*. Updated with a new chapter on the Age of Obama. Princeton, NJ: Princeton University Press, 2018.

Gibson, Arrell Morgan, ed. *Between Two Worlds: The Survival of Twentieth Century Indians*. Oklahoma City: Oklahoma Historical Society, 1986.

Hall, John A., ed. *The State of the Nation: Ernest Gellner and the Theory of Nationalism*. New York: Cambridge University Press, 1998.

Handlin, Oscar. *Race and Nationality in American Life*. Boston: Little, Brown, 1948.

Higham, John. "The Future of American History." *Journal of American History* 80 (1994): 1289–1309.

———. *Strangers in the Land: Patterns of American Nativism, 1860–1925*. New York: Atheneum, 1955, 1966.

Hobsbawm, E. J. *Nations and Nationalism Since 1780: Programme, Myth, Reality*. New York: Cambridge University Press, 1990.

Hollinger, David. "Nationalism, Cosmopolitanism, and the United States." In Pickus, *Immigration and Citizenship in the Twenty-First Century*, 85–99.

Ignatieff, Michael. *Blood and Belonging: Journeys into the New Nationalism*. New York: Viking, 1993.

Judt, Tony. "The New Old Nationalism." *New York Review of Books*, May 26, 1994.

Kazin, Michael. "A Patriotic Left." *Dissent*, October 1, 2002.

Kazin, Michael, and Joseph A. McCartin, eds. *Americanism: New Perspectives on the History of an Ideal* Chapel Hill: University of North Carolina Press, 2006.

Kedourie, Elie. *Nationalism*. London: Hutchinson University Library, 1960.

Kohn, Hans. *American Nationalism: An Interpretive Essay*. New York: Macmillan, 1957.

Lee, Erika. *The Making of Asian America: A History*. New York: Simon & Schuster, 2015.

Leeman, William P. "George Bancroft's Civil War: Slavery, Abraham Lincoln, and the Course of History." *New England Quarterly* 81 (2008): 462–88.

Levinson, Sanford. "Is Liberal Nationalism an Oxymoron? An Essay for Judith Shklar." *Ethics* 105 (1995): 626–45.

Lieber, Francis. *Nationalism: A Fragment of Political Science*. New York, 1860.

Lieven, Anatol. *America Right or Wrong: An Anatomy of American Nationalism*. New York: Oxford University Press, 2004.

Lind, Michael. "The Case for American Nationalism." *The National Interest*, May–June 2014.

———. *The Next American Nation: The New Nationalism and the Fourth American Revolution*. New York: Free Press, 1995.

McCardell, John. *The Idea of a Southern Nation: Southern Nationalists and Southern Nationalism, 1830–1860*. New York: Norton, 1979.

McCartney, Paul T. "American Nationalism and U.S. Foreign Policy from September 11 to the Iraq War." *Political Science Quarterly* 119 (2004): 399–423.

Maier, Charles. *Once Within Boundaries: Territories of Power, Wealth and Belonging Since 1500*. Cambridge, MA: Harvard University Press, 2016.

Minian, Ana Raquel. *Undocumented Lives: The Untold Story of Mexican Migration*. Cambridge, MA: Harvard University Press, 2018.

Murrin, John. "A Roof without Walls: The Dilemma of American National Identity." In Beeman et al., *Beyond Confederation*, 333–48.

Ngai, Mae M. *Impossible Subjects: Illegal Aliens and the Making of Modern America*. Princeton, NJ: Princeton University Press, 2004.

Offen, Karen, ed. *Globalizing Feminisms, 1789–1945*. London: Routledge, 2010.

Okrent, Daniel. *The Guarded Gate: Bigotry, Eugenics, and the Law That Kept Two Generations of Jews, Italians, and Other European Immigrants Out of America*. New York: Scribner, 2019.

Pask, Kevin. "Mosaics of American Nationalism." *New Left Review* 88 (July–August 2014): 69–87.

Pei, Minxin. "The Paradoxes of American Nationalism." *Foreign Policy*, May/June 2003.

Pfaff, William. *The Wrath of Nations: Civilization and the Furies of Nationalism*. New York: Simon & Schuster, 1993.

Pickus, Noah M. J., ed. *Immigration and Citizenship in the Twenty-First Century*. Lanham, MD: Rowman and Littlefield, 1998.

Poliandri, Simone, ed. *Nationalism and Nation Re-building in Native North America: Past and Present Cases*. Albany: State University of New York Press, 2016.

Potter, David M. "The Historian's Use of Nationalism and Vice Versa." *Journal of American History* 67 (1962): 924–50.

Renan, Ernest. "What Is a Nation?" In Ernest Renan, *Qu'est-ce qu'une nation?* Translated by Ethan Rundell. Paris: Presses-Pocket, 1992.

Roshwald, Aviel. *The Endurance of Nationalism: Ancient Roots and Modern Dilemmas.* New York. Cambridge University Press, 2006.

Sánchez, George J. *Becoming Mexican American: Ethnicity, Culture, and Identity in Chicano Los Angeles, 1900–1945.* New York: Oxford University Press, 1993.

Schlesinger, Arthur M., Jr. *The Disuniting of America.* New York: Norton 1991.

———. *The Vital Center: the Politics of Freedom.* Boston: Houghton Mifflin, 1949.

Smith, Rogers. *Civic Ideals: Conflicting Visions of Citizenship in U.S. History.* New Haven, CT: Yale University Press, 1997.

Snyder, Louis L. *The Meaning of Nationalism.* New Brunswick, NJ: Rutgers University Press, 1954.

Spencer, Philip, and Howard Wollman, eds. *Nationalism: A Critical Introduction*. London: Sage, 2002.

Sutherland, Claire. *Nationalism in the Twenty-first Century: Challenges and Responses*. New York: Palgrave Macmillan, 2012.

Tamir, Yael. *Liberal Nationalism*. Princeton, NJ: Princeton University Press, 1993.

Tolz, Vera, and Stephenie Booth. *Nation and Gender in Contemporary Europe*. Manchester: Manchester University Press, 2005.

Trautsch, Jasper M. "The Origins and Nature of American Nationalism." *National Identities* 18 (2016): 289–312.

Trilling, Lionel. *The Liberal Imagination*. New York: Viking, 1950.

U.S. Immigration Commission. *Dictionary of Races or Peoples*. Washington, DC: Government Printing Office, 1910.

Waldstreicher, David. *In the Midst of Perpetual Fetes: The Making of American Nationalism, 1776–1820*. Chapel Hill: University of North Carolina Press, 1997.

Wiebe, Robert H. *Who We Are: A History of Popular Nationalism*. Princeton, NJ: Princeton University Press, 2002.

Wong, Edlie L. *Racial Reconstruction: Black Inclusion, Chinese Exclusion, and the Fictions of Citizenship*. New York: New York University Press, 2015.